TELECOMMUNICATION NETWORKS - TRENDS AND DEVELOPMENTS

Edited by **Mohammad Abdul Matin**

Telecommunication Networks - Trends and Developments
http://dx.doi.org/10.5772/intechopen.75287
Edited by Mohammad Abdul Matin

Contributors

Natalia Vasilenko, Alexey Linkov, Asaad Ahmed, Rameez Asif, Bill Buchanan, Oleg V. Zemlyaniy, Konstantin Lukin, Kazu Okumoto, Rashid Mijumbi, Abhaya Asthana, Toto Saktioto, Roby Ikhsan

First published in London, United Kingdom, 2019 by IntechOpen
IntechOpen is the global imprint of INTECHOPEN LIMITED, registered in England and Wales, registration number: 11086078, The Shard, 25th floor, 32 London Bridge Street
London, SE19SG – United Kingdom
Printed in Croatia

British Library Cataloguing-in-Publication Data
A catalogue record for this book is available from the British Library

Additional hard copies can be obtained from orders@intechopen.com

Telecommunication Networks - Trends and Developments, Edited by Mohammad Abdul Matin
p. cm.
Print ISBN 978-1-78985-719-1
Online ISBN 978-1-78985-720-7

For EU product safety concerns:
IN TECH d.o.o., Prolaz Marije Krucifikse Kozulić 3, 51000 Rijeka, Croatia,
info@intechopen.com or visit our website at intechopen.com.

Meet the editor

Dr. Mohammad A. Matin currently works at the Department of Electrical and Computer Engineering, North South University, Bangladesh, as an associate professor. He obtained his BSc degree in Electrical and Electronic Engineering from BUET (Bangladesh), his MSc degree in digital communication from Loughborough University, UK, and his PhD degree in Wireless Communication from Newcastle University, UK. He has published over 90 refereed journals and conference papers and is the author of 14 academic books and 13 book chapters. He has presented invited talks in Bangladesh and Malaysia, and has served as a member of the program committee for more than 50 international conferences. Dr. Matin is currently serving as a member of the editorial board of several international journals such as IEEE Communications Magazine and IET Wireless Sensor Systems. He has received a number of prizes and scholarships, including the Best Student Prize (Loughborough University) and the Commonwealth Scholarship and Overseas Research Scholarship. His current research interests include UWB communication, wireless sensor networks, cognitive radio, and antenna engineering.

Contents

Preface

The demand for advance telecommunication services has increased dramatically over the last few years. This has led to technological changes with revolutionized engineering strategies to optimize network construction and operation. Telecommunication networks integrate with a wide range of technologies, including optical amplifiers, software architectures for network control and management, abstract algebra required to design error correction codes, and network modeling. This book presents research contributions towards new techniques, concepts, analysis of the telecom market's evolving trends, and infrastructure to provide integrated voice, data, and video communications services that are critical to the operation and competitiveness of companies, governments, and other organizations.

Chapter 1 presents the structure and dynamics of the main indicators of the Russian telecommunication services market for the growth of telecommunication companies. It takes into account its strong state protectionism, which is conditioned by the strategic importance and the high social significance of the telecommunications industry.

Chapter 2 describes the design challenges in optimizing a hybrid quantum-classical network and the initial results, based on experimental and numerical analysis, to characterize and evaluate the distribution of secure data to the subscribers using the Quantum-to-the-Home (QTTH) transmission model. The presented results provide a solid base to enhance the existing telecommunication infrastructure and modules to deliver end-to-end optical data encryption to subscribers.

Chapter 3 explores BRACE—a cloud-based, integrated, one-stop center for software reliability modeling, testing, and defect analysis. Each of these is provided as-a-service to development teams. Initial implementation of BRACE includes a software reliability growth modeling algorithm, which provides defect prediction for both early and late stages of the software development cycle. To illustrate and validate the tool and algorithm, the authors also discuss key use cases, including actual defect and outage data from two large-scale software development projects from telecom products.

Chapter 4 presents a concept of chaos-based physical layer protocol for secure communication and hidden data transmission over an open network channel. The protocol is based on spectral keying of chaotic signals generated by nonlinear dynamical systems with delayed feedback. In this technique, the modulating information sequence controls the parameter of nonlinear elements, so that it switches the chaotic modes and changes the spectral structure of the signal, which is transmitted to the communication channel.

Chapter 5 provides an overview of optical amplifiers. The optical amplifier is an important element in optical communication networks. Tremendous progress has been made recently in erbium-doped fiber amplifiers, semiconductor optical amplifiers, Raman amplifiers, and other types of optical amplifiers. In semiconductor optical amplifiers (SOAs), electron-hole recombination occurs, whereas in Raman amplifiers, Raman scattering of incoming light with phonons in the lattice of the gain medium produces photons coherent with the incoming photons. In this chapter, the authors did the simulation for both the amplifiers. The results showed that the transmission distance of the fiber Raman amplifier (FRA) is much further than the SOA shown by BER and Q-factor. However, this FRA system has higher power consumption when compared to the SOA system.

Chapter 6 attempts to introduce the benefits and challenges of the Internet of Things (IoT) for telecommunications networks.

It is believed that the students who seek to learn the latest advanced research in telecommunication networks will need this book.

Mohammad Abdul Matin
Department of Electrical and Computer Engineering
North South University, Dhaka, Bangladesh

Chapter 1

Customization of the Telecommunication Market Based on the Application of the Concept of Service Products

Natalia V. Vasilenko and Alexey J. Linkov

Additional information is available at the end of the chapter

http://dx.doi.org/10.5772/intechopen.79030

Abstract

The analysis of the structure and dynamics of the main indicators of the Russian telecommunication services market shows the achievement of saturation state of this market and the exhaustion of extensive sources of growth. Given the presence of a complex of negative socioeconomic factors, the source of maintaining the market positions of telecommunication companies is the customization of the services offered. For this purpose, the concept of the service products can be applied, involving the inclusion of the additional, accompanying and derivative services into the customer service package. The prerequisites for the application of the concept of the service product in the telecommunication field are the availability of the multiattribute properties and interdependence of elements in the product of that field. On the telecommunication market we can consider three types of service products. Customization of the Russian market of telecommunication services is carried out taking into account its strong state protectionism, which is conditioned by the strategic importance and the high social significance of the telecommunication industry. Saturation of the market in the conditions of oligopoly and sophistication of consumers stimulate the telecommunication companies to include in their market offer the service products of all three types.

Keywords: telecommunications, technologies, services, telecommunication services market, service product, customization, additional service, accompanying service, derivative service

1. Introduction

The economy and the society of the twenty-first century are functioning in the conditions of the rapidly developing telecommunication technologies. Their ubiquitous application accelerates the economic development, contributes to higher living standards and welfare of the population, and creates new sources of competitive advantages for the enterprises, industries and national economies in general.

In the modern conditions, the telecommunications industry belongs to one of the most strategically important sectors of the Russian economy, performing the infrastructural function of ensuring the needs of society in the transmission of various kinds of information. Advanced development of the telecommunications is a prerequisite for creating of the business infrastructure and the favorable conditions for investment attracting, for solving of the employment problems.

"The Concept for the Development of the Telecommunications Services Market in the Russian Federation" (http://www.inforeg.ru) identifies the main segments of the telecommunication services market:

- the mobile communication services, leading in the total volume of telecommunication services and characterized by a high level of competition in the conditions, on the one hand, of the steady growth of the number of Russian mobile subscribers (1.5–1.8 times per year) and, on the other hand, a steady decrease of the tariffs for the corresponding services;
- the local telephone services, whose operators concentrate their efforts on the attracting of the most solvent customers, offering a wide range of modern services;
- long distance and international telecommunication services that are monopolized by Rostelecom in Russia, but the operators of other communication networks can use some elements of the infrastructure of this company;
- the data transmission services (including the Internet), developing most rapidly compared to other segments of the telecommunications market in terms of subscribers growth and infrastructure development.

The Russian market of the telecommunication services reached a volume of 1672.0 billion rubles by 2015. According to data in **Table 1**, the share of the mobile communication services in the total volume of telecommunication services increases from 25.5 to 34.5% in the period of 2000–2015, gradually replacing the services provided by fixed telephones (from 53.9 to 11.7%, respectively). Even more clearly, this trend was manifested for services rendered to the population, for which the share of the mobile communication services increased from 26.6 to 54.8%, and the share of fixed communication decreased from 58.6 to 9.8%.

At the same time, the share of the mobile communication services has declined over the past 5 years in the total volume of telecommunication services from 43.8 to 34.5%, being replaced by Internet-based data services, whose share shows steady growth, reaching 16.1% by 2015.

It should be noted that over the past 10 years, the telecommunications market in Russia has reached its saturation. This process was due to two basic circumstances.

First, by the stabilization of the market structure in terms of the main types of consumers (see **Table 2**).

Second, by stabilization of the number of telephone sets of the public switched telephone network and mobile cellular subscribers (see **Table 3**).

	2000	2005	2010	2015
Total				
Mobile communication	25.5	42.9	43.8	34.5
Local telephone communication	21.9	16.0	11.7	7.8
Intercity, intrazonal and international telephone communication	32.0	11.9	8.1	3.9
Traffic connection	....	10.8	13.8	16.1
Other services	20.6	18.4	22.7	37.7
Services rendered to the population				
Mobile communication	22.6	63.8	70.5	54.8
Local telephone communication	26.5	17.8	11.4	8.2
Intercity, intrazonal and international telephone communication	32.1	9.7	4.8	1.6
Other services	18.8	8.7	13.4	35.3

Source: Calculated by "Transport and Communications in Russia". 2016: Stat.sb./Rosstat. – M., 2016. – 86 p.

Table 1. The Structure of the Russian telecommunications services market by main segment (the share in total volume, %).

	2000	2005	2010	2015
Share in the total volume of services rendered to business and the public sector	64.4	46.8	44.6	46.9
Share in the total volume of services rendered to the population	35.6	53.2	55.4	53.1

Source: Calculated by "Transport and Communications in Russia". 2016: Stat.sb./Rosstat. – M., 2016. – 86 p.

Table 2. The structure of the Russian market of the telecommunication services by main types of consumers (share in total volume, %).

	2005	2010	2013	2014
Number of telephones	29.9	31.4	28.9	26.8
The number of cellular subscribers	86.3	166.4	193.3	190.3

Source: Compiled by "Transport and Communications in Russia". 2016: Stat.sb./Rosstat. – M., 2016. – 86 p.

Table 3. The volume of telephone sets of public telephone network and mobile cellular subscribers in Russia (at the end of the year, per 100 population).

The preservation of the described trends in 2016–2017 is confirmed by the results of a study conducted by the Analytical Research "Russian Telecommunications Market–2017. Preliminary Results" made by Agency TMT Consulting (http://tmt-consulting.ru). In this study is the following expanded structure of the telecommunications services market presented: mobile communications–55%, Internet access–12%, postal services–10%, fixed telephony–8%, pay TV–5%, inter-operator services–4%, others–6% .

At present, the main providers of telecommunications services can be divided (with some degree of conventionality) into two groups, differing by the technologies used and by the set of telecommunication services provided (**Table 4**).

No	Type of provider	Types of services provided
1	Fixed-line operators	• local telephony, • long-distance and international telephone communication, • access to the Internet, • cable TV, • digital television, etc.
2	Cellular operators	• voice services, • data-services, • mobile Internet, • mobile on-line-services, etc.

Table 4. The main types of the telecommunication service providers.

The data in **Table 4** confirm that the development of the telecommunications services market is primarily due to the dissemination of the new technologies [1]:

- the mobile communication technologies supplant the fixed communication services due to the high level of competitiveness of the mobile communication and IP telephony;
- a wired connection is currently dominated in the Internet access. It is explained by the faster connection speed compared to a wireless connection, the ability to transmit the large amounts of information as well as a high degree of reliability and security;
- with the introduction of fourth and fifth generations of the technologies, which have a higher data transfer rate and lower delay in sending packets than 3G technology, a gradual decrease in the share of fixed communication and in the provision of data services is predicted.

Despite the fact that the technologies provide continuous improvement of the quality of telecommunication services, the key aspect of the market interaction between producer and consumer remains the process of the telecommunication services providing.

A number of negative factors can be identified for the further development of the Russian market of telecommunication services [2, 3]:

- a slowdown of GDP growth rates, a decrease in the income level of the population, which, in order to optimize the expenditures, reduces the consumption of services with the high elasticity, which require or the support by the telecommunication services, or the telecommunications services themselves;
- the saturation of the mobile communication services market, which means the exhaustion of opportunities for extensive development (there are 151 active subscribers per 100 population in Russia, which exceeds the level of the developed countries by a quarter (120)

and the level of the developing countries by two-thirds (91). Every second Russian visits Internet daily (https://issek.hse.ru);

- a steady tendency to reduce the average price per minute, which dropped in Russia from 2.23 rubles to 0.38 rubles in 2004–2014, as well as tendency to reduce the average price of 1 megabyte–from 21.43 rubles (2006) to 0.11 rubles (2014), which complicates the task of preserving the market positions of telecommunication services providers;
- shortening of the life cycle of technologies used in the telecommunications industry, leading to the need for substantial investment into the infrastructure changes at the threat of loss of the market positions;
- the sophistication of consumers requiring the high-quality service and attention to their desires from the mobile operators that offering essentially homogeneous products (in terms of minutes, SMS, megabytes). In these conditions, it is necessary to search for those sources of growth that will ensure the growth in revenue of mobile operators in the near future. To solve this problem, the authors consider promising the application of the concept of the service product.

2. Customization of the telecommunication market through the customization of the telecommunication service products

2.1. The concept of the service product

The basis for the formation of the concept of the telecommunication service product is a stable tendency to change the structure of the world economy in favor of the service sector. This major institutional change is accompanied by the fragmentation of the industrial monopolies into industrial and service components and leads to the complication of economic ties and relations in which the consumer begins to play an increasingly important role. Subjective assessment of the value of services and the technological achievements contribute to the individualization of consumption and as a response of producers to the needs of the market—to the customization of the production. The proposed concept of the service product allows to divide the value delivered to the consumer of services into its components and to orient service organizations to strategic product innovations.

The service product is an independent service or a system that combines the material products and related services [4].

The expediency of linking services and goods in a service product is confirmed by modern trends in the development of the service sector. First, the provision of a number of services involves the consumption of certain goods, items of material nature. At the same time, many material objects are closely tied to the services and only to the services. To obtain a mobile communication service [5], the consumer needs to purchase a special device (phone, tablet, etc.) and a SIM card that will allow using the communication service. With the development of technical progress, with the spread of high technology, this trend is increasing.

Second, the consumption of some goods is supplemented by the acquisition of accompanying services. Such an addition can increase the attractiveness of the goods for consumers. Therefore, the purchase of the smartphone becomes attractive, as it allows access to the Internet and to various mobile applications that allow the customer make purchases, manage financial resources, etc.

Third, the basic service is accompanied by the receipt of related goods and services [6]. For example, air passengers can receive the food, press, duty-free goods in the flight, baggage transportation services, etc. When staying at the hotel, the customer can order a taxi to the airport, tickets for the concert, etc. Modern Internet technologies allow almost any service to be accompanied by financial online operations.

An important property of the service product is its multiattributivity. The service product is a collection of many attributes with different properties and purposes. Therefore, one can single out in it a basic, or a primary utility, directly correlated with the satisfaction of the customer need, which has become an incentive for the purchase of the service product.

The customer can add to the primary utility the additional attributes that create additional or secondary utility and increase the beneficial effect for the consumer due to greater comfort, lower time costs, etc.

The additional attributes can be both functional (objective) and emotional (subjective) results of the perception.

In this case, the most important difference between the multiattributivity of the service product and the multiattributivity of a good is that for different consumers, the basic utility can be formed by various services and goods that are part of the same service product.

The multiattributivity of the service product and the "floating" (under the influence of consumer preferences) nature of the primary utility explain the second important property of the service product—the interdependence between all its parts. This interdependence determines the inclusion into the service product of the maximum possible (from the point of view of economic feasibility) number of attributes with the possibility of choosing the attribute which is important for the consumer.

To order the attributes of the service product, it is useful to divide them into two groups [7]:

- invariable attribute of the service product, without which the consumer cannot imagine the realization of the basic function (the primary perceived utility);
- variable attribute of the service product, the presence or absence of which will signal to the consumer about the class and status of the goods (secondary perceived utility).

In this case, as a rule, both basic and additional utilities are most often created and offered not by one firm, but by a group of participants of the industrial market [8]. This premise makes it possible to combine optimally the model of multiattributive goods with the model of the industrial "chain" of the added value creating, and, accordingly, of the utility creating.

The results of research in the field of the quality of services assessing [9–11] confirm that the degree of perception of the service product is formed for the consumer as a cumulative estimate of the consumption of all its components. The competition in the provision of the services, correlated with the primary utility, has already led to a situation where further improvement in their quality depends on the achievements of scientific and technological progress and significant investments. Therefore, the opportunities for gaining competitive advantages due to the perception of the consumer value of the service product are associated with the added components of it, which are variable from the point of view of the offer of various service organizations. This is about a secondary perceived utility.

To determine the composition of the service product in terms of the secondary perceived utility, it is advisable to consider three types of services [12]:

- additional services,
- accompanying services,
- derivative services.

The additional services can be divided into two groups:

- compulsory services, provided by the service organization, since their absence or poor quality adversely affects the final assessment of the consumer;
- noncompulsory services, fulfilling the role of strengthening of the consumer perception and giving a certain individuality to the service organization.

The accompanying services do not appear on the market as an independent object of purchase and sale. They are provided to consumers in the form of a free supplement as the price of the accompanying service does not appear as an independent part of the payment, but is included by the seller into the market price of the service product. The accompanying services act as the ensuring of the purchased product delivery to a location specified by the buyer, as the setting up or adjusting of the purchased product, as the providing of some additional information, as the training to use the purchased product, as the spare parts supplying, as the providing of the special guarantees, insurance services, etc.

The derivative services include the services, the availability of which is established by the rules for the provision of services preceding the derivative services in accordance with their nature and purpose. The need for derivative services arises in the conditions when the consumer receives the right to provide him with some kind of basic service. Together with this right, a potential opportunity to use a whole bunch of derivative services (of both paid and partially paid or already included into the price) is acquired.

The diversity and compatibility of the telecommunication services with other services, as well as with some material objects, for example, devices and equipment, create the prerequisites for the application of the concept of the service product for the telecommunications industry.

2.2. The types of telecommunication service products

In the Federal Law of the Russian Federation "On the Communications," the communication services are treated as the activities for receiving, processing, storing, transferring, and delivering of the messages by electricity connections or postal items. According to the all-Russian classifier of economic activity types, these services are included in the section "The activity in the field of the electricity connection" (Code 64.2 in the classifier of economic activity types, OKVED). In the conditions of the rapid development of information, electronic and digital technologies, the services in the field of the electricity connection are increasingly beginning to be considered as telecommunication services.

The term "telecommunications" comes from the Latin word "communico," which means "the form of communication," and from the Greek word "tele," which means "acting at a great distance." To date, telecommunications is a complex of methods for the transfer of information, which is based on the transmission and transformation of electromagnetic signals. From a technical point of view, the main type of a good produced by the telecommunications industry is the exchange of information at remote (and near) distances, which can take place in different forms, depending on the mode of transmission, the type of channel, and the type of signal.

From the economic point of view, the telecommunication service can be described by the benefits to the consumer. Such benefits are reflected in the attributes of the service [13]. The multiattributivity of the mobile communication service is shown in **Table 5**.

By selecting and combining the most important attributes for consumers, the telecommunication services provider attracts attention to them, forming a demand from potential customers. Depending on the predicted primary utility of a certain consumer segment, the values indicated in **Table 5** will be either invariant or variable.

The interdependence of the components of the service telecommunications product is manifested (in accordance with the neoclassical economic theory) in two aspects: interchangeability and complementarity.

The prerequisite for the interchangeability of the telecommunication services is the availability of various ways of the information conveying. Therefore, to send a message, it is possible to use a direct call, send an SMS or MMS message, write a letter by e-mail, leave a message in your voice mail, and so on.

The interchangeability of some ways of the information conveying leads to the emergence of new services on the market with improved quality parameters and to the decrease in the demand for traditional services. According to the reporting of telecommunication companies, the number of fixed telephony subscribers in Russia decreased by 0.8–1.0 million people per year in the period 2010–2013. More than 1.8 million subscribers refused to use mobile telephony services in 2015. The factor of pressure on the price of calls in the network of mobile operators, especially on the price of long-distance and international calls, is the VoIP system, which ensures the transmission of the voice signal over the Internet [2].

No	Title	Content
1	The technical quality of communication	• The quality of the voice transfer • The reliability and the speed of delivery of messages • The opportunity to call at any time • The breadth of coverage in the place of residence of the consumer and other settlements
2	The range of services provided by the mobile operator	• The differentiation of the services • The reliability in obtaining the necessary services • The ease of activation, use and cancelation of services
3	The level of consumer costs (tariffs)	• The differentiation of tariff plans • The simplicity and clarity of tariff plans • The total cost of mobile communications
4	The billing	• The update rate of the balance • The convenience of replenishment of the account and payment for the provided services • Accuracy and correctness of withdrawal of money from the account
5	Strategies for interaction with the consumers of services (CRM)	• The volume and methods of information providing • Availability of loyalty programs • A list of services that can be obtained through the automatic menu on the website • Availability and convenience of the call-center services

Note: compiled on the basis of the research data of the agency UMG–International.

Table 5. The mobile service attributes.

The development of one of the mutually complementary services in the telecommunications market ensures the activation of the demand for another service. Therefore, the drivers of the demand for SIM-cards of mobile operators at first were the voice services, then short messages without the need for an immediate response (SMS), and finally, mobile Internet traffic. However, it should be noted that the more and more subscribers start to use the special applications for data transfer, as the cost of traffic (megabytes) is cheaper than standard calls and SMS. The active development of wi-fi networks with free access replaces paid mobile Internet services.

The market of these services, in particular the market of mobile communication services, is a network market [14]. This fact is of a significant importance for the formation of the usefulness of the telecommunication services. This means that the utility of the service on the network market depends on its prevalence among the potential consumers. The positive external effect from the introduction of a new service or a new service product on the network market can be a result [15].

The primary and secondary perceived utilities of the telecommunication services product components can vary from one group of consumers to another. To cover a larger number of potential consumers, the companies that participate in the formation of the telecommunication service products use several strategies:

- the mobile device manufacturers supply them with numerous unified sets of built-in applications, giving the possibility to the consumer to expand these sets, individualizing the consumption;
- the mobile communication service operators, based on a constant analysis of the market situation of telecommunications services, differentiate the offer through the implantation of various combinations of homogeneous products into different tariff plans;
- the companies that provide other types of services using digital technologies and develop new services, for example, electronic store, electronic reservation system, mobile bank, mobile television, etc.

The service products from the point of view of the telecommunications industry participation in them can be divided into three types:

- internal, covering the products and services produced by enterprises and organizations of the telecommunications industry, for example, the services packages of mobile operators;
- external in terms of resources, including the necessary material elements, produced, in particular, by enterprises of the electrotechnical industry, for example, mobile phones, tablets, computers, etc.;
- external in terms of the target function that assumes that the consumer uses the telecommunication services product as a means of access to some basic good or service, for example, opening a deposit through a mobile bank or booking a table in a restaurant through a mobile operator.

Let us consider each type of service product in detail.

To characterize the internal telecommunications service products, the service package model [16] and the corresponding batch sales technology [17] can be applied.

In accordance with this approach, the product of the telecommunications industry is provided as a set of different services, which together form the aggregate service product, including (from the manufacturer's point of view).

- the main service for the providing of which the company-operator enters the market;
- auxiliary services that promote the consumption of the main service, so without them, the package cannot be sold to the consumer;
- supporting services aimed at increasing the attractiveness of the main service for consumers and creating the prerequisites for forming a competitive advantage of the company offering them.

If the main service provided by the company is the connection of a telephone, the Internet or a pay-TV, then the customer support, payment methods, etc. can be considered as the auxiliary services, and the training, the provision of information materials, etc., can be considered as supporting services.

The main advantage of the technology of the package sales is that the provision of a services package reduces sales costs due to economies of scale and the ability to use the discounts that exist in the company. Therefore, it is not necessary to reduce further the cost of telecommunications services. Therefore, this technology can be considered a non-price tool to increase the customer loyalty.

It is important to understand that from the positions of the customer and the performer of the telecommunication service product the designation of its components is not the same (**Table 6**), so that modern companies operating in the telecommunication services market, offering service packages of different substantive content, in some cases be combined with each other [18].

The data in **Table 6** confirm that the basis of the packet sales technology in relation to the internal telecommunication service products is detailed elaboration of proposals for the formation of packages of services with a justification of their composition for a variety of conditions (for different groups of customers).

The inclusion of telecommunication services to external in terms of resources telecommunication service products due to their dependence from the technology development, causing the improvement of the material components of the service product—devices and equipment (hard) and information and network infrastructure (soft). Thus, the external in terms of resources telecommunication service products include not only telecommunication companies' services but also products of the electronic industry and other industries, as well as the results of operations for the development of software and databases for the functioning of social networks.

Many achievements in the field of microelectronics, computer technology, space research, new material technologies and many others are immediately used to form new and to improve

On the part of the telecommunication services customer	On the part of the telecommunication services provider
1. The basic service that has the primary utility for the consumer, 2. The additional services: • compulsory, providing a standard level of technical quality of the service, • optional, focused on the individualization of the supply, 3. The accompanying services that create an increased level of consumer comfort in accordance with the customer's strategy, 4. The derived services, access to which the consumer receives when paying for the basic service.	1. The main service for which the company-operator enters the market; 2. The auxiliary services that technologically support the implementation of the main service; 3. The supporting services aimed at attracting of the consumers

Table 6. The structure of the telecommunication service product.

functioning technical and computing facilities, communication networks [19]. All this contributes to the emergence of new information technologies and meeting the needs for telecommunication services. Manufacturers of mobile devices determine the rate of development and modernization of the telecommunication services market because they supply the base stations, controllers and switching centers for cellular operators. For example, in Russia, the equipment for "Megafon" is mainly supplied by Nokia and Siemens; for "VimpelCom" –by Alcatel, Sony, Nokia; for MTS–by Siemens, Sony, Motorola.

According to Cisco's data, by 2017, about two-thirds of the world's mobile traffic falls to the share of smartphones (Cisco Visual Networking Index: Global Mobile Data Traffic Forecast Update, 2012–2017). Monthly traffic volumes per device increase from 342 to 2660 MB over the same period. From 2012 to 2017, the average speed of the mobile channel increases 7.4 times, and the average connection speed for smartphones and tablets increases 3.2 times. One of the main factors of this increase is the improvement of the technical characteristics of mobile devices.

The social networks are the main driver of the growth of mobile VoIP services. VoIP services are increasingly being built into the social networking applications that provide economic benefits for making international and long distance telephone calls, as well as for creating the distributed corporate telephone networks (**Table 7**).

Depending on the specifics of the formation of external in terms of resources telecommunication service products, the commodity policy of telecommunications companies should include the planning of an assortment of telecommunications equipment, without which it is impossible to provide the corresponding services. This allows not only to demonstrate the quality of service in the company but also to strengthen the "material component" of the service.

Some examples of the external telecommunications service products are as follows:

- sale of SIM-cards with USB-modems, telephone sets, routers and other equipment under the brand of a mobile operator,
- sell the service "Internet access" with modems under the brand of an Internet provider.

No	Service name	Features and possibilities
1	Skype–messenger, including on mobile platforms	• Making and receiving calls to ordinary phones • Provision of video communication and videoconferences up to 10 people
2	Google Hangouts–service for business communications, including on mobile platforms	• Application for group video communication (Meet) • Application for group chat (Chat)
3	Viber–mobile VoIP application for iPhone, integrates into the address book	• Making free calls in high quality between smartphones with Viber installed • Making calls to ordinary and mobile phones at low rates

Source: http://www.voipoffice.ru.

Table 7. The most common IP telephony services (VoIP).

Expediency of functioning on the market of the external in terms of the target function telecommunication service products is caused by infrastructural function of telecommunications in relation to other economy branches.

The telecommunications sector permeates in the modern conditions virtually all areas of the economic activity plays a leading role in the productions processes organizing, improving the efficiency of public administration, solving of security problems, and so on. This trend will increase with the development of the digital economy, which is based on the means of communications. The consumers will need not only the transfer of information in itself, as access to the various platforms and services in the electronic form. Hence, the development of the external in terms of the target function telecommunication service products is associated with the process of digitalization of the services.

The most important difference between the types of service products being considered from the other two types of service products is that the primary utility for the consumer can be associated with any service provided by digital technologies. The digital technology is a fusion of information technology and telecommunications. Telecommunication services that generate secondary utility can be a part of the additional, accompanying or derivative services. It will depend on the generated service product and the customer preferences (**Table 8**).

A special place in the external in terms of the target function telecommunication service products is occupied by financial services. In this case, the integration of two infrastructure functions is realized. The result of this process is the transfer of information for the movement of electronic funds, implying a change of their owner (e.g., in the case of payment for goods or services) or a change of their forms (e.g., in the situation of the credit deal).

The integrated component of the service product in this area is mobile banking as well as various payment systems. According to OKchanger.ru, the most popular payment systems are PayPal (24.32% user voices), Perfect Money (14.47%) and Payeer (11.74%).

The modern telecommunications companies have a direct impact on the customization of the service products of all types. This problem is discussed in the next section of the chapter.

No	The primary utility	The type of the economic activity	The role of the telecommunication services in the secondary utility	The type of the telecommunication services in the service product
1	Acquisition of the right to receive the service	the service at the pharmacy	electronic queue	additional (mandatory)
2	Acquisition of the right to receive services	the distribution of tickets for the entertainment events	on-line booking service	additional (optional)
3	Purchase of a good	e-commerce, logistics services	on-line services of the goods orders and their tracking	accompanying
4	Reception of the service	passenger transport	on-line registration service	derivative

Table 8. The examples of the structure of the external in terms of the target function telecommunication service products.

2.3. The features of the Russian telecommunication market and the customization of telecommunication service products

The customization is the adaptation of the mass products or services to the needs of the individual consumer. At the core of customization lies the individualization of consumer demand, prepared by the development of modern technology, which created the prerequisites for personifying of the service conditions.

The personalization of the supply requires the increasing of the telecommunication industry companies' flexibility, which could not be achieved in the conditions of the natural monopoly, classically justified for the communications industry. The experience of many countries shows that the modern telecommunication services market is undergoing the transformation toward imperfect competition. This market is an oligopoly in Russia (**Table 9**).

Currently, the Russian telecommunications market is formed by four main public corporations with 80% of the market approximately: "MTS," "Megafon," "VimpelCom" (brand "Beeline," currently within the EON Ltd. group of companies), and "Rostelecom." These companies are actively competitive among themselves within the whole period of their existence.

On the Russian telecommunications market, there are also several dozens of independent mobile phone operators. The largest is "T2 Mobile (Tele2)"company, which is in the competition with the "big three" of federal operators. However, ComNews Research analysts agree that the market share of the independent mobile phone operators will be reduced in the future in favor of the federal level players.

An important feature of the Russian telecommunication services market is the State protectionism, which manifests itself in the foreign investment restricting into the telecommunication industry, which the Russian government considers as strategic industry [20].

The main tasks of the government policy in the sphere of telecommunications in Russia can be as follows:

- the improvement of the system of regulatory legal regulation of the industry aimed at developing of telecommunication services market;
- the construction of modern national telecommunications infrastructure;
- the development of the competitive environment in the telecommunications market;
- the increasing of the telecommunications industry investment attractiveness;
- the development of new technologies supporting telecommunication services;
- the integration of the Russian telecommunication complex into the European and world telecommunication complexes taking into account national interests.

Another important feature of the Russian telecommunication services market is their social significance, generated by numerous external effects, including the effects in the field of personal and public security [21]. For these purposes, the concept of universal service has been formed in the regulatory framework. Such a service is characterized as

No	The sign name	The sign demonstration	
		In the conditions of a natural monopoly	**In the Russian telecommunication market**
1	The Supply Formation	One company	Several communication operators
2	The service substitutes	None	Differentiation of services and service products
3	The barriers to entry	High barriers are associated with significant institutional constraints	The weakening of the institutional and technological barriers
4	The source to low the average costs	Increase of the volume of service supply	Constant updating of the technologies used by new market participants

Table 9. The comparative analysis of the signs of the natural monopoly and oligopoly in relation to the Russian market of telecommunication services.

a certain minimum set of services of an established quality that are accessible to all users regardless of their geographical location at an acceptable price, established depending on certain national conditions. A universal service is a minimum guaranteed telecommunications service product. Universal service does not imply the customization, being essentially mass.

The high level of competition, the saturation of the market and the sophistication of consumers stimulate telecommunication companies to differentiate their supply. However, the copying of the claimed components of the service product leads to the fact that gradually a number of services are offered by the majority of participants in the telecommunications market, for example, the services of the promised payment or the possibility of changing the mobile operator with the maintaining of the mobile phone number. In this situation, the advantage is gained by the market participant who realizes more efficiently the customization of the service products offered to the consumer.

The formation of the service products allows to solve the following tasks to telecommunication companies [16]:

- to provide the consumers with discounts on services, tariffs for which are regulated by the state;
- to differentiate the standard set of the telecommunication services;
- to develop a wide range of niche offers, which is economically unjustifiably when they are individually representing at the market. At the same time, the service products may differ in the possibility of price management, the form of payment and the composition of the services provided in the service product.

The service products can perform on the telecommunications market in the following forms:

- integrated service packages [22], combining the voice services and the DATA-services in the tariff plans for at a fixed monthly fee, which provides a guaranteed return for the company;

- asymmetrical packages [23], covering the service with low profitability that leads in terms of customer loyalty, and driven high profitability service with low consumer loyalty.

The use of service products in the form of integrated packages of services from the point of view of the consumer is essentially the purchase of services in bulk (a single tariff including voice, Internet, text messaging), which is much cheaper than connecting services separately. For sales offices of telecommunications companies, the implementation of integrated packages is also convenient, since in this situation they offer a single integrated package of service. Previously, in addition to sell the basic service, it was also necessary to sell additional options, depending on the client needs.

In the service product, created in the form of an asymmetric package of services, the differences between the leading and the driven services, which are usually very noticeable when sold separately, are smoothed out. A leading service with the high loyalty can level out the low loyalty for slave, profitable service, when the consumer is interested in acquiring the leading service in any form, either separately or as part of a service product. Thus, such a service product increases customer loyalty primarily to a profitable service, as its consumption grows with the growth in sales for a "leader" service. As a result, the total revenue on two services, taken separately, is less than the revenue for the service product. The application of the concept of the service product developing for the telecommunication services market in the three types of telecommunications service products should take into account the following trends in changes in consumer preferences in the current state of technologies:

- the availability of any of the services regardless of the location of the consumer;
- the receiving of the content "on demand", in particular, as a mobile video, the share of which in 2017, according to Cisco, was 66.5% of total mobile traffic, compared with 36% in 2012;
- access to the gaming capabilities of mobile devices, especially smartphones.

To strengthen the market positions, the telecommunications companies should:

- to introduce the new technologies to improve the quality and to reduce the cost of services;
- to increase the share of the supply of service products of these types, depending on the preferences of the telecommunication services consumers;
- to create the strategic alliances for the expanding of the resource capabilities to offer not only internal, but also external telecommunication service products in terms of resources and of the target function.

3. Conclusion

Currently, the development of the Russian market of telecommunication services, associated with the dissemination of the new technologies, is constrained by the population decrease of the revenues, the need for significant investments to the infrastructure change, by the reduction in average prices per minute and per transfer of one megabyte of data and by increasing the exactingness of consumers of the telecommunication services.

Despite the fact that the technologies provide the continuous improvement of the quality of telecommunication services, the key aspect of interaction between the customers and the companies is currently the characteristics of the customer service process. In the conditions of saturation of the telecommunications services market, customization can be achieved through the formation and supply of the service products. By combining a set of products and services, the service product allows to satisfy simultaneously the needs of various groups of consumers due to the "floating" nature of the primary and secondary perceived utilities, as well as due to the interdependence of the invariant and variable attributes of the service product. In terms of secondary utility in the service product, it is necessary to distinguish additional, accompanying and derivative services.

From the economic point of view, the telecommunication service can be described by the benefits to the consumer, reflected in the invariant and variable attributes of the service. These attributes are combined in the service products in such a way to ensure demand on the basis of maximum possible compliance with consumers' expectations. The interchangeability of telecommunications services, due to the availability of various methods of the information transferring, usually leads to the emergence of new services on the market with improved quality parameters. Complementarity of services in the telecommunications market is supported by its network nature.

The "floating" nature of the primary utility and the digitalization of the economy led to the formation of three types of the service products involving telecommunications services. Domestic telecommunications products, formed on the basis of packet sales technology, combine products and services produced by enterprises and organizations of the telecommunications industry. The external telecommunication service products in terms of resources include the provision of equipment and mobile applications, including the network applications. To ensure this, the telecommunications companies, as a rule, have their own online stores. They also introduce themselves into the social resources network.

The prerequisite for the formation of the external telecommunication service products in terms of target function is the digitization of services in the modern economy. It is these services that represent the primary utility for the consumer. The telecommunication services can form the secondary utility for the consumer when they are a part of the service product together with the additional, accompanying, derivative services.

The main characteristics of the modern Russian market of telecommunication services should be considered the transition from a natural monopoly to an oligopoly, a strategic character of the telecommunication services market to ensure the implementation of state interests, the social significance of this market. The main forms of customization of the telecommunication services market offer are integrated and asymmetric packages of services.

The development of service products of all types plays an important role to increase the performance of telecommunication companies' activity. It is the service products that are the tools that make it possible to increase in the modern market conditions the attractiveness of both telecommunications services and telecommunications companies themselves for existing and potential customers.

Author details

Natalia V. Vasilenko[1]* and Alexey J. Linkov[2]

*Address all correspondence to: nvasilenko@mail.ru

1 Saint-Petersburg Minining University, Saint-Petersburg, Russian Federation

2 Russian State Herzen Pedagogical University, Saint-Petersburg, Russian Federation

References

[1] Suhanov PS. Perspektivnye napravlenija razvitija mirovogo rynka telekommunikacij [Prospective directions of development of ohe world telecommunications market]. Vestnik of the Plekhanov Russian University of Economics. 2013;**11**(65):102-109

[2] Sigarev A, Kosov M. Threats to competitiveness of Russian telecommunication companies in modern economy. Financial Life. 2016;**4**:4-8

[3] Yang Y, Yang B, Humphreys P, McIvor R, Cadden T. An investigation into E-business service in the UK telecommunication manufacturing industry. Production Planning & Control. 2017;**28**(3):256-266. DOI: 10.1080/09537287.2017.1280622

[4] Oskina TA. Conditions of occurrence and the tendency of developing of service economy. RISK: Resources, Information, Supply, Competition. 2009;**2**:177-181

[5] Kibkalo JV. Organizacionno-jekonomicheskoe obespechenie standartov telekommunikacionnyh uslug [Organizational and Economic Support of Telecommunication Services Standards]. Samara: SGJeU; 2012. 25 p

[6] Kiselev SV, Shakirov MM. Soderzhanie, harakteristika i klassifikacija telekommunikacionnyh uslug kak ob#ekta issledovanija. [The content, characterization and classification of the telecommunication services as a research object]. Bulletin of Kazan Technological University. 2013;**16**(10):311-316

[7] Neretina TG. Organizacija servisnoj dejatel'nosti [Organization of Service Activities]. Moskva: FLINTA; 2014. 102 p

[8] Mumuni AG, Luqmani M, Quraeshi ZA. Telecom market liberalization and service performance outcomes of an incumbent monopoly. International Business Review. 2017;**26**(2):214-224

[9] Gronroos CA. Service Management and Marketing: Customer Management in Service Competition. 3nd ed. Chichester: John Wiley & Sons; 2007

[10] Parasuraman A, Berry LL, Zeithaml VA. Conceptual model of service quality and its implications for future research. Journal of Marketing. 1985;**49**(4):41-50

[11] Zeithaml VA, Parasuraman A, Berry LL. Problems and strategies in services marketing. Journal of Marketing. 1985;**49**:33-46

[12] Rajzberg BA. Vvedenie v jekonomiku uslug [Introduction to the Services Economics]. Moskva: MPSU; 2014. 152 p

[13] Dagli O, Jenkins G. Consumer preferences for improvements in mobile telecommunication services. Telematics and Informatics. 2016;**33**(1):205-216. DOI: 10.1016/j.tele.2015.07.002

[14] Chung JH, Yoo TH. Government policy, network externalities and mobile telecommunication services: Evidence from OECD countries. Applied Economics. 2015;**47**(21):2173-2183. DOI: 10.1080/00036846.2015.1005816

[15] Kokovihin AJ, Ogorodnikova ES, Plahin AE, Pavlova AV. Strategicheskie al'ternativy rynka sotovoj svjazi Rossii. Jekonomika: teorija i praktika [Strategic alternatives to the cellular market in Russia]. Economics: Theory and Practice. 2017;**3**(47):42-46

[16] Fedotov AV. Marketingovye aspekty razvitija rynka telekommunikacionnyh uslug [Marketing Aspects of Development of the Market of Telecommunication Services]. Moskva: Publishing house of Nasirddinova V.V; 2012. 52 p

[17] Granaturov V, Kaptur V, Politova I. Determination of tariffs on telecommunication services based on modeling the cost of their providing: Methodological and practical aspects of application. Economic Annals-XXI. 2016;**156**(1-2):83-87. DOI: 10.21003/ea.V156-0019

[18] Chen LK, Yang WN. Perceived service quality discrepancies between telecommunication service provider and customer. Computer Standards & Interfaces. 2015;**41**:85-97. DOI: 10.1016/j.csi.2015.02.012

[19] Alzami S, Shakya S, Boyd I. Transforming telecommunications service execution. Journal of The Institute of Telecommunications Professionals. 2017;**11**:22-26

[20] Tarasova OY, Pakhomova YV. Influence of current trends of development of the Russian market of telecommunications on financial management of the enterprises of cellular communication. Social and Economic Phenomena and Processes. 2015;**10**(8):124-130

[21] Milne C, Batura O. Liberalisation of telecommunications services: Social embedding of the liberalised market as a regulatory challenge. In: Batura O, editor. Universal Service in WTO and EU Law: Liberalisation and Social Regulation in Telecommunications. Berlin: Springer; 2016. pp. 11-61. DOI: 10.1007/978-94-6265-081-7_2

[22] Perevoznikova MV. Clustering criteria of cellular communication market. Vestnik of Astrakhan State Technical University. Series: Economic. 2015;**4**:49-55

[23] Makarov VV, Bershev SM, Aliev NM. Metodika adaptivnogo upravlenija potrebleniem uslug, predostavljaemyh v sostave paketov [The method of adaptive management of the consumption of services provided in the package]. Journal of Creative Economy. 2009;**11**:79-87

Chapter 2

Recent Progress in the Quantum-to-the-Home Networks

Rameez Asif and William J. Buchanan

Additional information is available at the end of the chapter

http://dx.doi.org/10.5772/intechopen.80396

Abstract

For secure data transmission to the end users in a conventional fiber-to-the-home (FTTH) network, quantum cryptography (QC) is getting much consideration nowadays. QC or more specifically quantum key distribution (QKD) promises unconditionally secure protocol, the Holy Grail of communication and information security that is based on the fundamental laws of quantum physics. In this chapter, we discuss the design issues in a hybrid quantum-classical communication network, performance of the cost-effective off-the-shelf telecommunication equipment, our latest results on a four-state (Quadrature Phase Shift Keying, 'QPSK') RF sub-carrier assisted continuous-variable quantum key distribution (CV-QKD) multiuser network based on ultra-low loss quantum channel (pure silica core fiber, 'PSCF') and microelectromechanical systems (MEMS) based add/drop switch. The results are thoroughly compared with the commercially available high-cost encryption modules. It is expected that the discussed cost-effective and energy efficient QKD network can facilitate the practical applications of the CV-QKD protocol on the commercial scale in near future for smart access networks.

Keywords: quantum communications, optical fiber networks, telecommunication, encryption, security, privacy

1. Introduction

Fiber-to-the-home (FTTH) networks, also known as last mile broadband segment, have the required potential to match the huge capacity of data networks with the next-generation connectivity demands. Major telecommunication investments in FTTH infrastructure are expected for the next decade, with many initiatives already launched around the globe, driven by the new bandwidth hungry services and the necessity by the operators to deploy a future-proof infrastructure to maintain the quality of service (QoS). The FTTH world is taking shape and, as it does so, researchers are emphasizing much more on the network design and proposing the specific applications [1, 2]. Next-generation (NG) services to deploy a smart city concept, such as cloud computing, machine-to-machine (M2M) communications, Drone-of-Things (DoT) and Internet-of-things (IoT), require high-capacity optical fiber infrastructure as a backbone. According to the statistics, high-speed data traffic is increasing at a rate of 30–40% every year [3], around the globe. For this very reason, the M2M/IoT applications will not only benefit from fiber-optic broadband, they will require proper security and privacy in these networks. Both M2M and IoT are using the Internet to transpose the physical world onto the networked one, with many interconnected devices communicating autonomously. This bandwidth demand forces the network providers to adopt fiber-based last-mile connections and raising the challenge of moving access-network capacity to the next level, 1–10 Gbits/s data traffic to the home [4]. The researchers believe that FTTH is the key to develop a sustainable future in terms of smart city infrastructures, as a matter of fact, it is the only available state-of-the-art technology, when it comes to providing unprecedented bandwidth, multiuser data capacity, high-speed data transfer, consistency, secure communications and expendability.

With progressively more people using the smart IoT electronic devices and multiple-sensors, data security and privacy are the areas of exploration, concerned with shielding the inter and intra-connected electronic devices and networks in the infrastructure. Data encryption on the signals in transit, either it is from the devices to the base station or from the base station to the cloud, is the vital component of cybersecurity in the next-generation networks. It provides a physical layer of defense that shields confidential and private data from the external hackers. The most secure and widely used algorithms to protect the confidentiality and integrity are developed on symmetric cryptography methods. Much amended security is delivered with a mathematically indestructible form of encryption known as one-time pad [5]. In this method, the information is secured by using accurately random sequence of the identical length as the original transmitted data. In both classical and new algorithms for data encryption, the main functional challenge is to securely share the generated keys between the two parties, namely, sender (Alice) and receiver (Bob). Quantum key distribution (QKD) methods address these challenges by using quantum properties to exchange the secret information, that is, cryptographic key, which can then be used to encrypt messages that are being transmitted over an insecure public channel.

QKD is a method used to assign encryption keys between two nodes, that is, Alice and Bob. The unconditional security of QKD is established on the intrinsic laws of quantum mechanics [6, 7]. Any eavesdropper (i.e., commonly known as Eve or hacker) on the public communication channel attempting to obtain the information between Alice and Bob will interpose the quantum state of the encrypted data and thus can be noticed by the users as defined by the noncloning theorem [8] by monitoring the disruption in terms of quantum bit error rate (QBER) or excess noise. The exploration for long distance and equally high bit-rate quantum encrypted data transmission using optical fibers [9] has led researchers to evaluate the range of methods [10, 11]. Two classical methods were developed and implemented for encrypted transmission over a standard single mode fiber (SSMF), that is, DV-QKD [12, 13] and CV-QKD [14–16]. DV-QKD protocols, such as the famous BB84 or coherent one-way (COW) [17], involve the generation and detection of very weakly powered optical signals, ideally at the single photon level. A range of successful technologies has been implemented via the DV-QKD protocol, but typically these are quite different in terms of the equipment required from the technologies that are used in classical communications [18]. CV-QKD protocols have therefore been of attention as these protocols can make use of conventional telecommunication equipment and additional resources are not required at all. Moreover, the secure keys are randomly encoded on the quadrature of the coherent state of a light signal [19]. Such technique has the potential advantages because of its capability of attaining high secure key rate with modest technological resources and advancements in the network infrastructure.

During the last few years, there is an increasing trend to use CV-QKD to send encrypted data over public communication channels, as listed in **Table 1**. The main purpose is to adopt the classical equipment, that is coherent receiver that can be installed for dedicated photon counting [20]. The quadrature of the calibrated received signals is observed by implementing a balanced optical coherent receiver either using the homodyne or heterodyne method. The nonavailability of much advanced reconciliation signal processing techniques at low SNR values implies the restrictions on the transmission distance of CV-QKD networks to 60 km, which is lower than that of DV-QKD [21]. The resultant secure key rates of CV-QKD network are restricted by the bandwidth of the coherent receiver, electronic circuitry for analogue-to-digital conversion (ADC) and the performance of reconciliation schemes as signal post-processing algorithms. The net performance of the system is degraded by the excess noise that affects the optical signals at the high data rates [22, 23].

In this chapter, we discuss the design challenges and the initial results, based on experimental and numerical analysis, to characterize and evaluate the distribution of secure data to the subscribers by implementing the quantum-to-the-home (QTTH) concept. We have systematically studied the design challenges and the analysis of using: (1) phase-encoded data, that is,

Sr #	Reference	Protocol	Receiver Bandwidth	Repetition Rate	Transmission Distance	Secure Key Rates
1	J. Lodewyck et al. (2005)	Gaussian	10 MHz	1 MHz	55 km	Raw key rate up-to 1 Mbits/s
2	B. Qi et al. (2007)	Gaussian	1 MHz	100 kHz	5 km	30 kbits/s
3	Y. Shen et al. (2010)	Four-State	100 MHz	10 MHz	50 km	46.8 kbits/s
4	W. Xu-Yang et al. (2013)	Four-State	N/A	500 kHz	32 km	1 kbits/s
5	P. Jouguet et al. (2013)	Gaussian	N/A	1 MHz	80.5 km	0.7 kbits/s
6	S. Kleis et al. (2015)	Four-State	350 MHz	40 MHz	110 km	40 kbits/s
7	R. Kumar et al. (2015)	Gaussian + Classical	10 MHz	1 MHz	75 km	0.49 kbits/s
8	D. Huang et al. (2016)	Gaussian	5 MHz	2 MHz	100 km	500 bits/s
9	S. Kleis al. (2016)	Four-State	350 MHz	50 MHz	100 km	40 kbits/s
10	Z. Qu et al. (2016)	Four-State	23 GHz	2 GHz	back-to-back	$\geq$12 Mbits/s

Table 1. Overview of recent CV-QKD demonstrations.

m-PSK (where m = 2, 4, 8, 16 ….) to produce secure quantum keys and (2) limitations of using fast optical receivers in-terms of electronic and shot noise for commercially available coherent receiver to detect the CV-QKD signals. Furthermore, the transceivers, noise equivalent power (NEP) from ADCs and transimpedance amplifier (TIA) are emulated according to the physical parameters of the available off-the-shelf modules. Both single channel (suitable for high-speed point-to-point links) and especially wavelength division multiplexed (WDM) transmissions (suitable for multicasting) are investigated. We have also implemented: (1) local local oscillator (LLO) method to avoid possible eavesdropping or hacking on the reference laser signal and (2) a phase noise cancelation (PNC) algorithm for digital post-processing of the received signals. Moreover, we have depicted the trade-off between the secure key rates achieved and the split-ratio of the access network considering the hybrid classical-quantum traffic. The proposed set-up is further studied by incorporating different fiber types, for example, pure silica core fiber (PSCF) and low loss switch based on microelectromechanical systems (MEMS) for multiuser configurations. These detailed discussions will help the people from academics and industry to implement the QTTH concept in real-time networks. Furthermore, the designed system is energy efficient and cost-effective.

2. Theory and mathematical modeling

The complete mathematical model, as depicted in **Figure 1**, for generating quantum signals and the post processing algorithms are discussed in this section.

2.1. CV-QKD signals

At the transmitter, Alice produces pseudo-random m-PSK symbols that can be controlled via pseudorandom binary sequence (PRBS), that is, I(t),Q(t) $\in \{-1, +1\}$. These randomly generted symbols are up-converted to radio-frequency (RF) signal levels with respective in phase and quadrature [25], that are denoted by S_I (t) and S_Q(t). These two parts can be mathematically expressed as in Eqs. (1) and (2).

$$S_I(t) = I(t)\cos(\omega_1 t) - Q(t)\sin(\omega_1 t) \quad (1)$$

$$S_Q(t) = I(t)\sin(\omega_1 t) - Q(t)\cos(\omega_1 t) \quad (2)$$

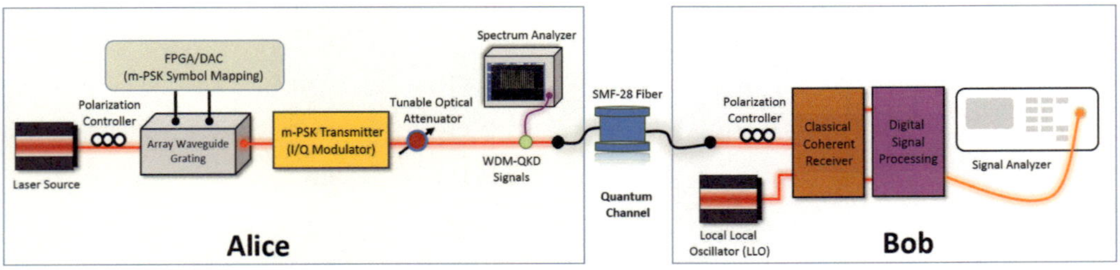

Figure 1. Schematic of the m-PSK-based quantum transmitter (Alice) and quantum receiver (Bob) for QTTH applications.

where $\omega 1$ is the RF angular frequency of the signal. The output is used as the input of I/Q modulator, Mach-Zehnder modulator (MZM). The equivalent optical field can be expressed as in Eq. (3) and further be simplified as in Eq. (4).

$$E(t) = \left\{ \cos\left[AS_1(t) + \frac{\pi}{2}\right] + j\cos\left[AS_Q(t) + \frac{\pi}{2}\right] \right\} \sqrt{P_s} e^{j[(\omega t + \varphi_1 t)]} \tag{3}$$

$$E(t) \simeq \sqrt{2P_s} e^{j[(\omega t + \frac{j\pi}{4})]} - A[I(t) + Q(t)]\sqrt{2P_s} e^{j[((\omega + \omega_1)t + \varphi_1 td)]} \tag{4}$$

where A refers to the modulation index; ω, P_S, and $\varphi_1 t$ represent the angular frequency of the carrier, power and phase noise of the received signal. For investigating, the modulation variance VA of the optical received signal, evaluated as the shot-noise-units (SNUs), the parameter A and variable optical attenuator have been optimized at the input of the public communication. To further simplify the numerical model of the QTTH network, the quantum channel loss is expressed as the attenuation of the optical communication channel. Mathematically, noise variance produced by the communication channel is given as in Eq. (5).

$$\chi_{line} = \frac{1}{T} + \epsilon - 1 \tag{5}$$

where T is the relationship between transmission distance and ϵ is the excess noise. Realistically, excess noise measurements, expressed as SNUs [18, 32], may come from the laser phase noise, laser line width, imperfect modulation and coherent receiver imbalance [33]. In this chapter, we have implemented a local local oscillator (LLO) concept, which is considered as the vital configuration to keep the laser at the receiver side, that is, Bob, in order to stay away from any hacking attempt on the quantum channel to get the reference phase information of the incoming signal. The electric field of the LLO can be expressed as in Eq. (6).

$$E_{LLO}t = \sqrt{P_{LLO}} e^{j[\omega_{LLO}t + \varphi_2 t]} \tag{6}$$

where P_{LLO}, ω_{LLO} and $\varphi_2 t$ represents the power, angular frequency and phase noise of the LLO, respectively. The structure of the Bob, that is, coherent receiver, consists of a 90° optical hybrid and two balanced photodetectors. The coherent receiver has an efficiency of η and electrical noise of V_{el}. Practically, V_{el} comprises electrical noise from transimpedance amplifiers (TIA) as well as the major contribution from the ADC. For this reason, the receiver added noise variance can be expressed as in Eq. (7).

$$\chi_{det} = \frac{2 + 2V_{vl} - \eta}{\eta} \tag{7}$$

Furthermore, the aggregate noise variance of the quantum network, including Alice and Bob, can be expressed as in Eq. (8).

$$\chi_{system} = \frac{\chi_{line} + \chi_{det}}{T} \tag{8}$$

2.2. Phase noise cancelation algorithm

Conventionally, in order to receive and process the weak quantum signals, a high-level local oscillator is required at the receiver. It is very vital to select the local oscillator with narrow line width so that the laser fluctuations cannot contribute to the overall system's excess noise that may damage the recovery of quantum signals. Furthermore, it will help the coherent receiver to have a low complex digital signal processing (DSP) module, that is, phase noise cancelation (PNC) algorithm, as explained in detail in **Figure 2** [25]. For the efficient performance of the PNC module, it is essential that the photocurrents of the in phase and quadrature signals have to be measured with high precision.

Mathematically, they can be expressed as in Eqs. (9) and (10).

$$\begin{aligned} \iota_I(t) \propto \sqrt{2}\cos\left[\omega - \omega_{LO})t + \varphi_1 t - \varphi_2 t + \frac{\pi}{4} - AI(t)\cos\left[(\omega + \omega_1 - \omega_{LO})t + \varphi_1 t - \varphi_2 t\right] \\ + AI(Q)\,cos\left[(\omega + \omega_1 - \omega_{LO})t + \varphi_1 t - \varphi_2 t\right] + n_I \end{aligned} \tag{9}$$

$$\begin{aligned} \iota_Q(t) \propto \sqrt{2}\sin\left[\omega - \omega_{LO})t + \varphi_1 t - \varphi_2 t + \frac{\pi}{4} - AI(t)\cos\left[(\omega + \omega_1 - \omega_{LO})t + \varphi_1 t - \varphi_2 t\right] \\ + AI(Q)\,sin\left[(\omega + \omega_1 - \omega_{LO})t + \varphi_1 t - \varphi_2 t\right] + n_Q \end{aligned} \tag{10}$$

where n_I and n_Q describe the in phase and quadrature components of the additive phase noise that needs to be remunerated. We have implemented the phase noise cancelation (PNC) algorithm [25]. By combining the squares of the in phase and quadrature component of photocurrents, as in Eqs. (9) and (10), that is, $i^2_I(t) + i^2_Q(t)$, and mitigating the DC component, the final result can be depicted as in Eq. (11).

$$\begin{aligned} \iota_S(t) \propto 2\sqrt{2}AI(t)\cos\left(\omega_1 t - \frac{\pi}{4}\right) + 2\sqrt{2}AQ(t)\cos\left(\omega_1 t - \frac{\pi}{4}\right) \\ + 2\sqrt{2}\left\{n_I\cos\left[(\omega - \omega_{LO})t + \varphi_1 t - \varphi_2 t + \frac{\pi}{4}\right] + n_Q\sin\left[(\omega - \omega_{LO})t + \varphi_1 t - \varphi_2 t + \frac{\pi}{4}\right]\right\} \end{aligned} \tag{11}$$

The final step in the DSP module is to down-convert the RF signal. The resultant in phase and quadrature components can be expressed as in Eqs. (12) and (13).

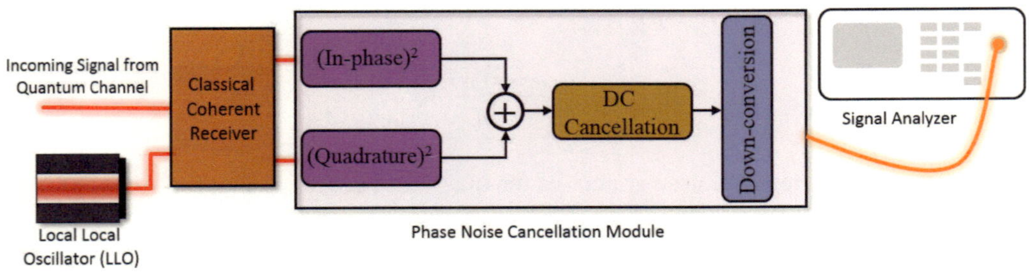

Figure 2. Schematic of the digital signal processing (phase noise cancelation) module for quantum receiver.

$$r_I = LPF\left[\iota_s(t)\cos\left(\omega_1 t - \frac{\pi}{4}\right)\right] = -\sqrt{2}AI + n'_I \tag{12}$$

$$r_Q = LPF\left[\iota_s(t)\sin\left(\omega_1 t - \frac{\pi}{4}\right)\right] = -\sqrt{2}AQ + n'_{IQ} \tag{13}$$

where n'_I and n'_Q are the equivalent additive noise that is added during the quantum channel transmission and detection processes before the digital post-processing. By considering Eqs. (12) and (13), it is determined that the original m-PSK signals can be recovered without any frequency and phase distortions.

3. Design of a hybrid quantum-classical network

In this section, we discuss the design challenges to optimize a hybrid quantum-classical network. More specifically, we discuss all the excess noise contributions, expressed as shot-noise-units (SNUs) [18, 32] may come from the imperfect modulation, laser phase noise, laser line width, local oscillator fluctuations and coherent detector imbalance [33].

3.1. Transmitter design

The design of the simplified QTTH network with m-PSK (where m = 4, 8, 16, etc.) modulation-based quantum transmitter (Alice) and LLO-based coherent receiver (Bob) is as shown in **Figure 1**. At Alice, a narrow line width laser is modeled at the wavelength of 1550 nm having a line width of approximately <5 kHz allowing it to maintain low phase noise regime. A pseudorandom binary sequence (PRBS) of length 2^{31}–1 is programmed for single channel transmission and delay decorrelated duplicates copies are generated for the multichannel transmission. Furthermore, we execute pulse shaping at the transmitter according to the Nyquist criterion to generate intersymbol interference (ISI) free signals. Subsequently, 1 GBaud 4-PSK (four state phase-shift keying) signal is generated after the radio frequency (RF) signals are modulated with the help of an electro-optical I/Q modulator, where RF frequency is kept at 2 GHz. The modulation variance is applied with the help of a variable optical attenuator (VOA) prior to the quantum channel, that is, based on the optical fiber.

3.2. Quantum channel

For most of our numerical and experimental investigations, we have used two standard types of fibers, namely, standard single mode fiber (SSMF) and pure silica core fiber (PSCF). The physical parameters of the fibers are given in **Table 2**. These are the commercial fibers and deployed heavily around the globe for short and long range transmissions. Therefore, these fibers can be used to benchmark the hybrid quantum-classical optical networks.

3.3. Classical coherent receiver

A standard commercially available coherent receiver has been modeled. The receiver module (Bob) consists of a 90° optical hybrid and 20 GHz balanced photodiodes. The gain of TIA,

	PSCF	SSMF
Fiber Loss (dB/km)	0.149	0.21
Aeff (μm^2)	135	80
Dispersion (ps/nm.km)	21.0	16.9
Dispersion Slope ($ps/nm^2.km$)	0.061	0.059
Macro-Bending Loss (R=10 mm) dB/m	4	7

Table 2. Physical characteristics of the fiber at 1550 nm.

responsivity and noise equivalent power (NEP) of the receiver at 1550 nm are 4 K.V/W, 0.8 A/W and 22 pW/pHz, respectively. For our analysis, we have kept the high-power laser at the receiver, that is, integral part of Bob in order to avoid any eavesdropping or hacking on the reference signal. That is why, it is termed as local local oscillator (LLO). The LLO photon level is considered as 1×10^8 photon per pulse. A phase noise cancelation (PNC) [25] based algorithm is implemented to minimize the excess noise as shown in **Figure 2(c)**. The PNC stage has two square operators for in phase and quadrature operators of the light signal, and a digital DC cancelation stage, assisted by a down-converter. The comprehensive implementation of the PNC module is described in Section 2.2 [25].

3.4. Characterization of coherent receiver

As a first step, we investigated the coherent receiver to detect the m-PSK signals as it is well known that the specific modulation formats require a very particular optical signal-to-noise ratio (OSNR) in order to be detected at a bit error rate (BER) threshold. After the modulation stage, the 4-PSK and 8-PSK signals, back-to-back signals are detected at the coherent receiver and normalized signal-to-noise ratio (Eb/N0, the energy per bit to noise power spectral density ratio) is plotted against BER. The results are plotted in **Figure 3(a)**. The BER threshold is set to be 3.8×10^3 (Q-factor of $\approx$ 8.6 dB), corresponding to a 7% overhead, that is, hard-decision forward error correction (HD-FEC). While soft-decision FEC (SD-FEC) level of BER 2.1×10^2 (Q-factor of $\approx$ 6.6 dB) can also be used corresponding to 20% overheard. From the results, we can depict that the minimum of 10 dB and 6 dB Eb/N0 values is required for the 8-PSK and 4-PSK signals at HD-FEC. While this limit can further be reduced to smaller values but at the cost of 20% overheard in data rates, that is, SD-FEC.

We have summarized the ADC requirements to detect the m-PSK signals. The results are as shown in **Figure 3(b)**. The ADC resolution (bits) is analyzed with respect to the SNR penalty for 1- and 4 GBaud m-PSK modulated signals. From the results, it is clear that 6–8 bit ADC can be installed in the network to recover the noisy m-PSK signals at diverse baud rates while keeping the SNR penalty $\approx$ 1 dB. Despite the well-known fact that high-resolution ADC can

http://dx.doi.org/10.5772/intechopen.80396

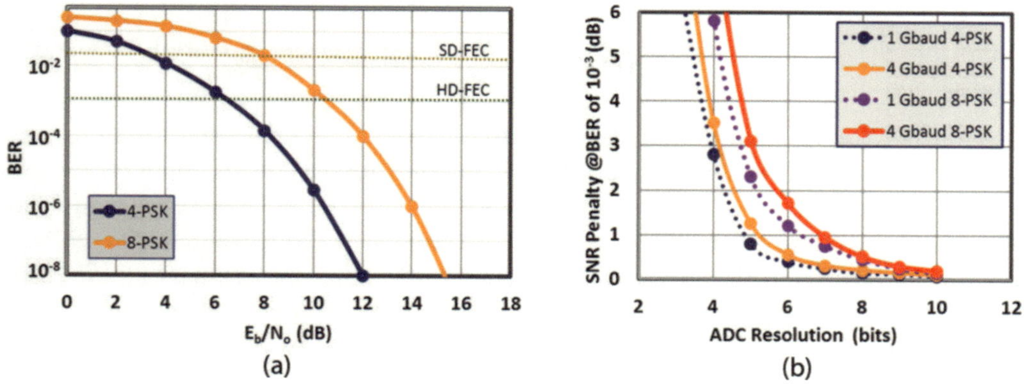

Figure 3. Performance comparison of classical data transmission: (a) averaged SNR with respect to m-PSK signals at different FEC levels and (b) SNR penalty with respect to ADC resolution for different baud rates for m-PSK signals.

Sr #	Modulation	ADC Bandwidth	ADC Sampling Rate ($T_s/2$)
1	4-PSK (4 Gbaud)	4 GHz	8 GS/s
2	8-PSK (4 Gbaud)	4 GHz	8 GS/s
3	8-PSK (2.66 Gbaud)	2.66 GHz	5.33 GS/s

Table 3. Summary of the ADC minimum requirements to process the m-PSK signals.

give efficient performance, they have high electronic noise that is not beneficial for quantum signals, that is, impacting the high secure key rates. The ADC requirements [24] in terms of bandwidth and sampling rate (Ts/2) are enlisted in **Table 3**.

4. Numerical analysis and discussions

4.1. Point-to-point QKD network

Since the noise equivalent power (NEP) determines electronic noise of the coherent receiver and digital post processing unit, it is important to choose a TIA and ADC with lower NEP values for low aggregate electronic noise to shot noise ratio (ESR). Furthermore, as the NEP of the TIA is amplified by the TIA itself (gain amplifiers), it governs the total electronic noise. However, the ESR negligibly changes as the bandwidth of the detector is increased. This is because of the fact that both electronic and shot noise variances linearly increase with the bandwidth, so it is advantageous to use the receivers having 1–20 GHz bandwidth. Since, 20 GHz receivers are easily commercially available so we have modeled them for our investigations. Furthermore, the quantum channel includes the standard SMF and VOA to model the channel loss. The variance of the excess noise is largely due to the bias fluctuation of the I/Q modulator and timing jitter of the Bob, that is, receiver modules. It is estimated that the excess noise can be limited to be as small as 0.01 [25] below the zero key rate threshold. After optimizing the transmission model: (1) the corresponding power is approximately −70 dBm (approximately 7.8×10^6 photons per pulse) [26], (2) the detector efficiency is 60% and (3) reconciliation efficiency is 95%.

Based on the abovementioned values, we extended our studies to calculate the secure key rates (SKR) at different transmission distances, that is, transmittance values. The input power is the same for every evaluation. Furthermore, SKR for both the 4-PSK and 8-PSK modulation formats under collective attack [22] are shown in **Figure 4(a)**. The maximum of 100 Mbits/s SKR can be attained with this simple configuration by using the commercially available modules for transmittance (T) =1 for 4-PSK modulation. While SKR of 25 Mbits/s and 1 Mbit/s at T = 0.8 and 0.6, respectively. From the results, it can also be concluded that the maximum transmission distance for CV-QKD-based network is 60 km. Hence, it is recommended that this QKD protocol can effectively be used for access network, that is, QTTH. We have also investigated the performance of 8-PSK modulation and the results are plotted in **Figure 4(a)**. The transmission performance is affected as compared to 4-PSK modulation, and this is due to the PNC algorithm that is executed to post-process the received quantum signal. This concept of generating seamless quantum keys can further be improved for multichannel networks that will help to generate high aggregate SKR via diversely multiplexing the neighboring quantum channels either by time, space, wavelength or polarization. In this chapter, we have multiplexed 12 WDM quantum channels to generate the aggregate SKR with the minimum channel spacing of 25- and 50 GHz. The WDM-QKD results, based on 4-PSK modulation, are shown as in **Figure 4(b)**.

The results depict that the classical multiplexing techniques can efficiently be used to multiplex quantum signals without any degradation in the SKR. We have multiplexed the signals by using 25- and 50 GHz channel spacing. Also, aggregating secure key rate can reach upto 1.2 Gbits/s for a 12 WDM quantum system at T = 1. The importance of these results are due to the fact that next-generation PON services are already aiming at Gbits/s data rates, so QKD can match the data rates. The 50 GHz channel spaced system depicts insignificant performance degradation as compared to single wavelength transmission. However, the 25 GHz channel

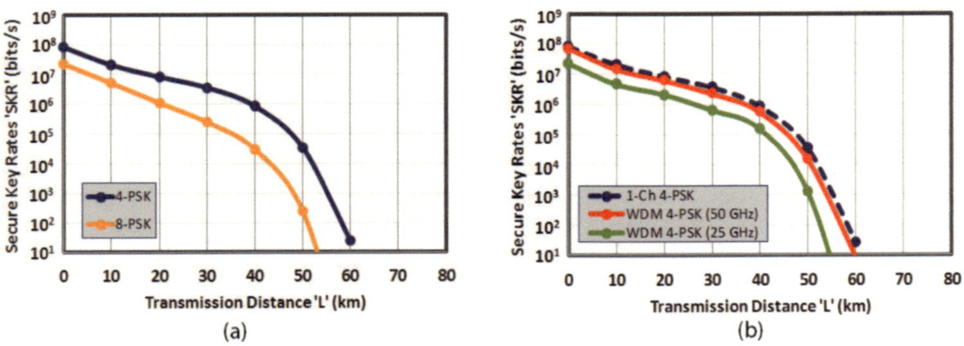

Figure 4. Calculated QKD with respect to transmission distance for: (a) 4-PSK and 8-PSK modulation and (b) single channel (1-Ch) 4-PSK modulation, 12 channel WDM 4-PSK modulation with 25 and 50 GHz channel spacing. (Note: Simulations are performed by assuming 60% detector efficiency and 95% reconciliation efficiency).

spaced system shows loss in SKR due to the impact of intersymbol interference between the adjacent neighboring channels.

The best available resource to mitigate the artifacts from the low-quality signal is to use raised-cosine filters for the pulse shaping at the transmitter. We can infer from the analysis that the quantum signals are compatible and ideal with classical optical add-drop multiplexers (OADMs) but the insertion loss from these modules can impact the SKR. A comparison of distance and secure key generation rate between CV-QKD using 20 GHz receiver and state-of-the-art DV-QKD systems based on T12 protocol [27, 28] is shown in **Figure 5**. The transmission distance of CV-QKD systems is limited than for DV-QKD demonstrations. However, comparative analysis of DV-QKD and CV-QKD shows that CV-QKD has the required performance to offer higher speed secure key transmission within an access network area (100 m to 50 km). Especially from 0 to 20 km range, that is, typical FTTH network, the SKR generated by using the traditional telecommunication components are 10s of magnitude higher than that of DV systems.

4.2. QTTH network

Most of the efforts on the QKD system design and experimental demonstrations are limited to laboratory environments and point-to-point transmissions. While actual FTTH networks have in-line optical devices including but not limited to routers, switches, passive splitters, add-drop multiplexers, erbium-doped fiber amplifiers (EDFA), as envisioned in **Figure 6(a)**. This restricts the deployment of QKD networks along with the classical data channels. However, in this chapter, we have investigated the compatibility of optical network components and their impact on the secure key rates. We have emulated the scenario of a typical quantum access network as shown in **Figure 6(b)**.

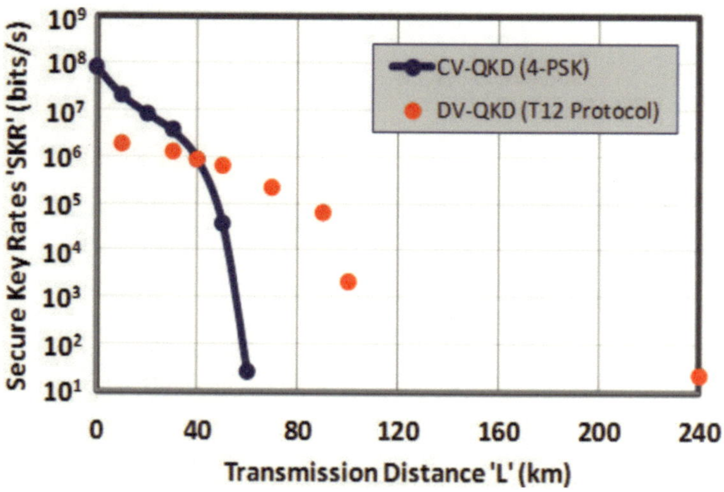

Figure 5. Performance comparison of CV-QKD vs. DV-QKD for access and metro networks.

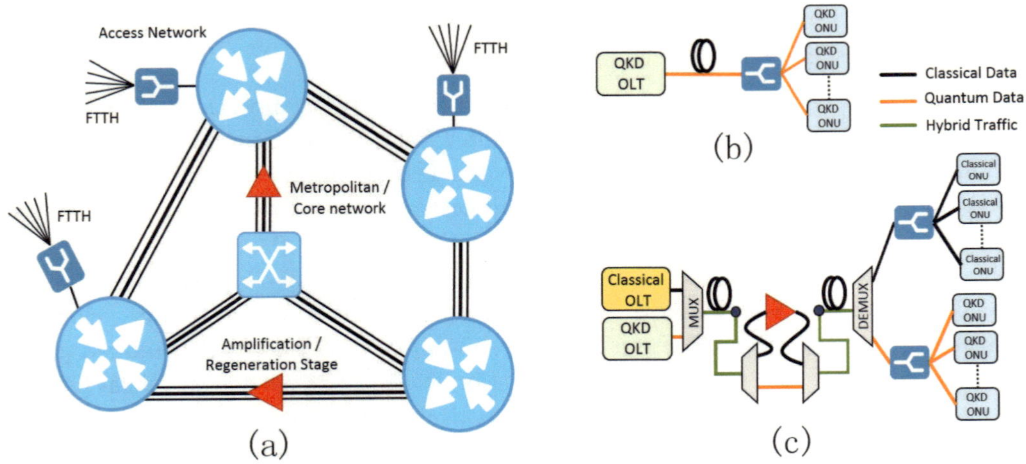

Figure 6. (a) Deployment of FTTH network with classical optical components; (b) downstream and upstream quantum access network and (c) hybrid classical-quantum traffic in access networks.

The optical line terminal (OLT) consists of a QKD transmitter, that is, in this chapter a m-PSK modulated transmitter is modeled. The optical distribution comprises as follows: (a) standard single mode fiber of 5 km length and (b) passive optical splitter with different split ratios. The commercially available splitters have insertion loss that is listed in **Table 4**.

The variable splitting ratio is vital for the secure key rates as it will contribute to the attenuation and excess noise of the system. To test the simulation model under realistic conditions, we have also added 0.15 dB splicing loss for every connection with the passive optical splitter. The results are depicted in **Figure 7** where we have plotted the SKR with respect to the splitting ratio of the system. It can be deduced from the graph that for a 1 × 2 splitting ratio, the SKR drops down to 10 Mbits/s per user while the SKR of 1 Mbits/s can be achieved with the splitting ratio of 1 × 4. Moreover, the classical telecommunication components can be used to design a seamless QTTH network and for short-range transmission as well as for data center applications it can perform better as compared to the much expensive DV-QKD systems [10].

Sr #	Split Ratio	Average Loss (dB)
1	1×2	3 dB
2	1×4	7.5 dB
3	1×8	11 dB
4	1×16	14.2 dB
5	1×32	17.8 dB
6	1×64	21.1 dB
7	1×128	23.8 dB

Table 4. Summary of the average attenuation (dB) associated with the standard passive optical splitters.

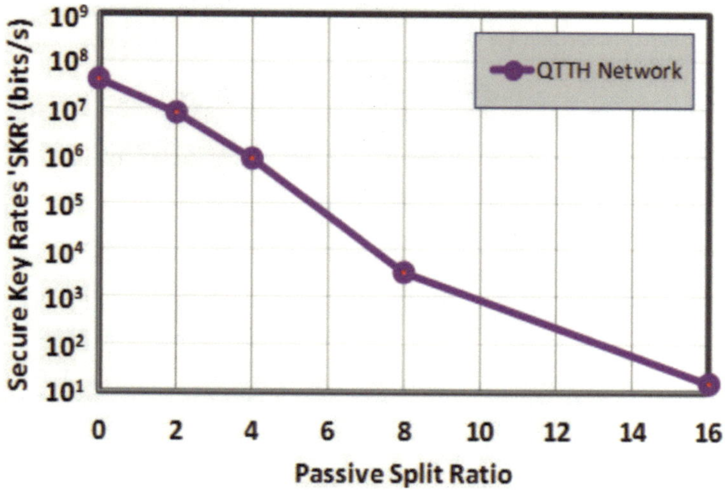

Figure 7. Performance comparison of QTTH network with diverse passive split ratios as a function of achieved.

4.3. Hybrid classical-quantum traffic in access networks

For the commercial compatibility of quantum signals with the existing optical networks, the wavelength and optimum power assignment to the signals are very much important. Different wavelength assignment [29–31] techniques have been investigated to avoid possible intersymbol interference between the classical and quantum signals. The best possible solution is to place the classical channels at 200 GHz channel spacing [31] in order to avoid any interference with the weakly powered quantum signals. Most importantly, we have implemented the concept of LLO, hence local oscillator signal is not generated from transmitter by using 90:10 coupler [18]. So apparently with LLO and 200 GHz channel spacing, there is no cross-talk among the hybrid classical quantum signals in the quantum channel. This is very much ideal for commercially available telecommunication components in the C-band (1530–1565 nm). Furthermore, with 200 GHz channel spacing, the classical channels can be encoded up to 400 Gbits/s line rate with advanced modulation formats, that is, dual-polarization m-QAM (m = 16, 32, 64 ….). But all-important thing is, high data rate classical channels need sophisticated high bandwidth receivers that inherently have high electronic noise. For this reason, they are not suitable for quantum multiplexed signals as shown in **Figure 6(c)**. As we are investigating a 20 GHz coherent receiver, so we have kept the data rate at 2.5 Gbits/s/polarization of quadrature phase-shift keying (QPSK) signals for classical data. The power of the classical data channels is optimized below −15 dBm. The quantum channel loss in this analysis corresponds to the 20 km of the optical fiber. The results for quantum signals at diverse wavelengths are depicted in **Figure 8**. The wavelength windows that are not occupied with the quantum channels are used for classical data transmission of QPSK signals. These signals are efficiently detected below the HD-FEC level. While the SKR of the quantum signals is 10 Mbits/s. We can conclude from the results the compatibility of quantum signals with the classical telecommunication components. Furthermore, L-band (1565–1625 nm, extended DWDM band) can also be used to generate the hybrid classical-quantum signals as broadband lasers are readily available commercially.

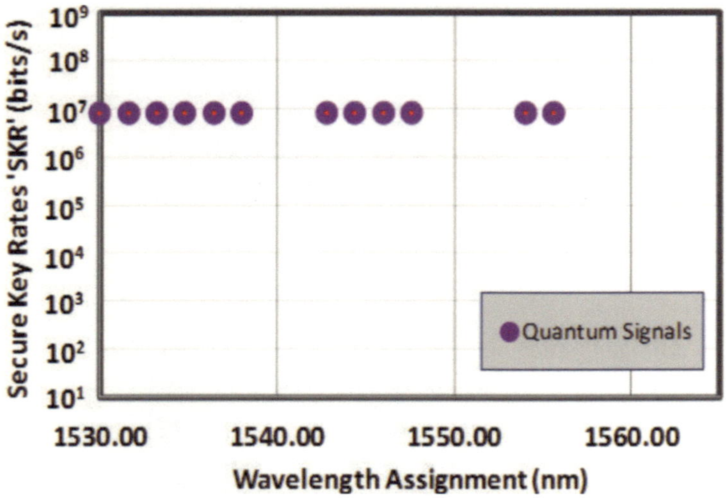

Figure 8. Optimum system performance and wavelength assignment for hybrid classical-quantum transmission.

5. Channel optimization for enhanced secure key rates

5.1. Experimental setup

The experimental setup for QPSK-based RF-assisted CV-QKD transmission is shown in **Figure 9(a)**. For the transmitter (Alice), a laser with narrow line width is operated at the wavelength of 1550.5 nm with a line width of <50 kHz permitting it to preserve the low phase noise characteristics. The PRBS of length 2^{31}–1 is programmed for single wavelength quantum transmission. Resultant 1 GBaud QPSK (four-state) signal is generated after the radio

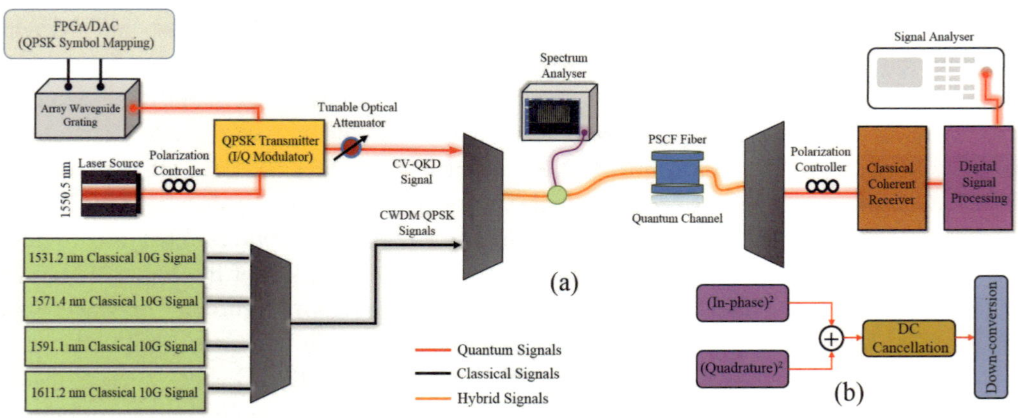

Figure 9. (a) Experimental set-up for point-to-point QPSK-based quantum transmitter (Alice), quantum channel and quantum receiver (Bob) with hybrid classical 10G traffic and (b) Digital signal processing module for phase noise cancelation (PNC) for quantum signals.

frequency (RF) signals are modulated via an electro-optical I/Q modulator, where RF frequency is kept at 2 GHz. The modulation variance (VA) of the generated quantum signal is optimized by a tunable optical attenuator (TOA). As it is a hybrid classical quantum network, therefore classical 10 Gbits/s QPSK channels are multiplexed at 1531.2, 1571.4, 1591.1 and 1611.2 nm wavelengths. All the classical data channels are optimized at 0.5 mW input power. Whereas, multiplexers and de-multiplexers have −45 dB of isolation between the two adjacent channels, −80 dB isolation between nonadjacent channels and 0.85 dB of insertion loss at 1550 nm. The quantum channel comprises pure silica core fiber (PSCF) with different transmission lengths (maximum = 35 km) and the physical parameters of the fiber under test are enlisted in Section 3.2. The system performance of QKD network is also compared with the SSMF fiber in terms of secure key rates and transmission distance, while Alice and Bob architectures are the same in both the cases.

The coherent receiver (Bob) consists of a 90° optical hybrid, a high optical power handling balanced photo-diodes with 20 GHz bandwidth and a real-time oscilloscope with a 100 GSa/s sample rate and 50 GHz analog bandwidth. We have kept the high power, narrow line width local oscillator at the receiver. It is termed as local local oscillator (LLO). The mean LLO photon level is 1×10^8 photon per pulse. The line width of the LLO is <10 kHz. After the system calibration at room temperature, the detector efficiency is measured as 0.6, while the electrical noise V_{el} is 0.85 (in shot noise units). The shot noise variance No is determined with sufficient LLO power to set the balanced detector in the linear detection regime. Shot noise calibration can be performed by shutting down all sources of incoming light or by ceasing the signal optical port on Bob side. The measured No for our setup is ≈17 0 mV2. The output signal is processed by the off-line digital signal processing module comprises phase noise cancelation (PNC) algorithm as depicted in **Figure 9**. The PNC stage has two square operators for in phase and quadrature operators, one addition operator and a digital DC cancelation block assisted by a down-converter. While all the secure key rate measurements are concluded with reconciliation efficiency of 90% for diverse modulation variances and transmission distances [30].

The extended experimental set-up for multiuser optically switched QKD network is shown in **Figure 10**. A MEMS-based 2 × 2 switch is incorporated after the quantum channel and demultiplexing, to implement inserted- and by-pass operations. The insertion loss of the switch is measured as 0.8 dB, while the cross talk (XT) is −52 dB, that is, negligible. In a by-pass state, the input and output ports are connected to each other and in inserted state, the input and drop ports are connected to each other. In order to recover the classical 10 Gbits/s signals, we have used a standard coherent receiver with built-in DSP module of finite-impulse response filters (FIR) to compensate chromatic dispersion (CD). The forward error correction (FEC) threshold is kept at 3.8×10^3 BER (bit error ratio).

5.2. Results and discussions

We evaluated the average SKRs for diverse modulation variances and transmission distances. While for this investigation, we use two types of quantum channel, that is, SSMF and ultra-low loss PSCF. The results are as shown in **Figure 11(a)** and **(b)**, respectively. Modulation variance is considered as 0.2, 0.3 and 0.4, while the length of quantum channel is considered upto 35 km

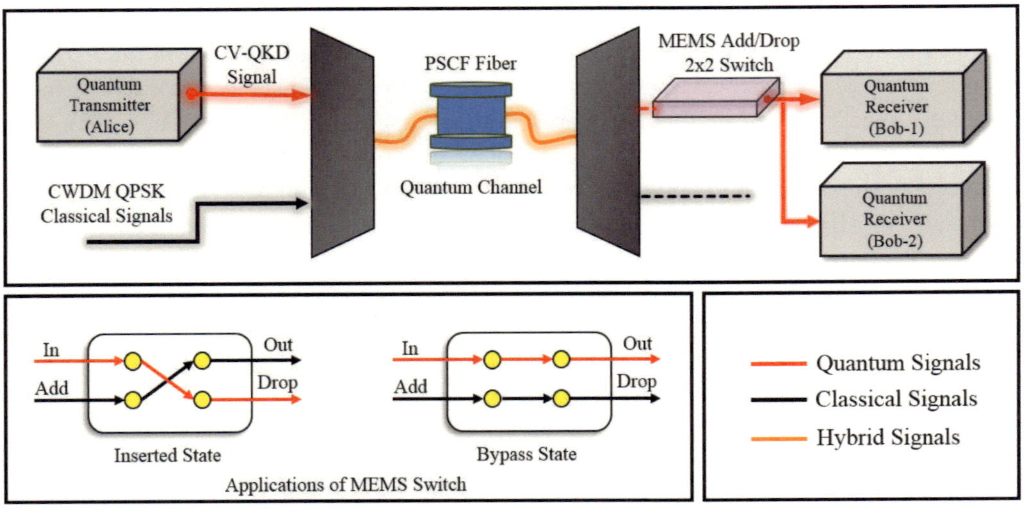

Figure 10. Experimental setup for multiuser optically switched quantum network incorporating 2 × 2 MEMS add/drop switch for implementing inserted and bypass cases along with hybrid classical 10G traffic.

maximum due to the limitations of resources in the laboratory. The maximum SKRs of 8.65 Mbit/s can be obtained with ultra-low loss PSCF-based quantum channel at 20 km transmission distance, as shown in **Figure 11(b)**. It can be seen that for the same transmission distance with SSMF-based quantum channel (**Figure 11(a)**), the average SKRs are reduced to 5.9 Mbit/s. It is evident from the results that the ultra-low loss PSCF-based quantum link can give you enhanced transmission distance with much improved key rates. It is worth mentioning here that since we are talking about the low baud rate signals and access networking distances, that is, 20–30 km, therefore PSCF fiber is performing better than SMF. It will be necessary to have dispersion mitigation module along with phase noise cancelation module as an integral part of Bob over much longer distances due to higher dispersion factor of PSCF fiber. It is further noticed that all the classical 10G channels are detected below the FEC threshold level, that is,

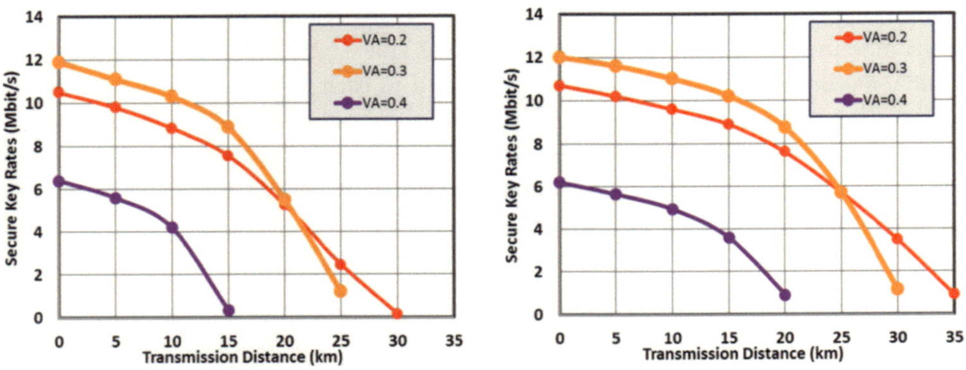

Figure 11. Experimental secure key rates (SKRs) measurements for diverse modulation variance values with respect to transmission distance for: (a) standard single mode fiber (SSMF) and (b) low loss pure silica core fiber (PSCF). The detector efficiency is 60% and reconciliation efficiency is 90%.

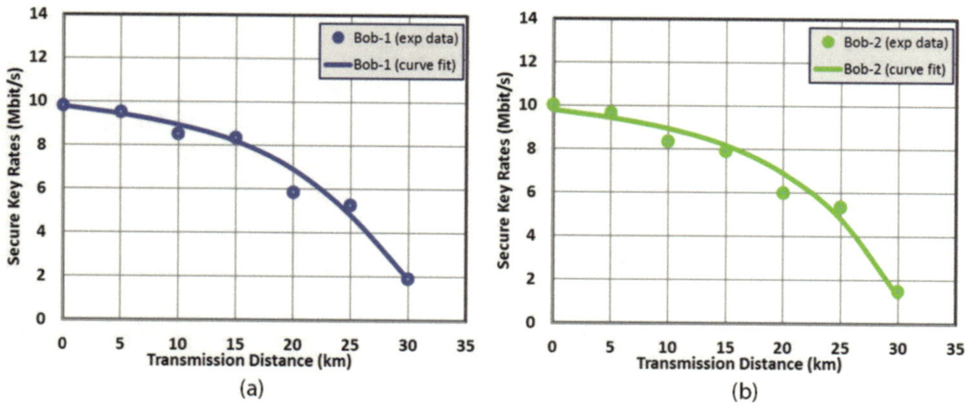

Figure 12. Experimental secure key rates (SKRs) measurements for multiuser optically switched QKD network with: (a) by-pass operation and (b) inserted state operation.

3.8×10^3 BER and due to the CWDM channel spacing, we have not seen any inter channel cross talk between the classical and weak quantum channels.

As we have stated earlier that till date, CV-QKD demonstrations are limited to point-to-point transmission between two distant nodes. For future integration of QKD networks with smart access networks, it is necessary to design a network that can transmit secure keys between multiple parties, hence optical switching techniques may be applied between QKD end-points. Since QKD is very much sensitive to insertion less, noise and cross talk, therefore in our experiment we have investigated a 2×2 MEMS-based switch with measured insertion loss of 0.8 dB, while the crosstalk (XT) is < -52 dB, that is, negligible and switching time is 20 ms. This is a two position device, that is, insertion and by-pass state as shown in **Figure 10**, that is commonly termed as optical add-drop multiplexer. In the by-pass operation, the input and output ports are connected to each other, that is, Alice is connected to Bob-1. On the other hand, in insertion operation, the input and drop ports are connected to each other, that is, Alice is connected to Bob-2, while at the same time, we can connect the add and output port for different set of secure keys. We have achieved 5.98 Mbit/s of secure key rates for almost both of the inserted and by-pass state at 20 km transmission distance, as in **Figure 12**. We certainly believe that in multiuser QKD network the optically switched key rates can further be improved with efficient splicing/coupling with same matching fiber, since in our case the MEMS 2×2 switch has 9/125 μm single mode fiber. Nevertheless, this key rate is much higher than the recently reported results of 4.75 Mbit/s for 1.5 dB attenuation (corresponding to 7.5 km quantum channel). The results discussed in this section are helpful to develop quantum secure routers that require high secure key rates, switching speed and low loss QKD optical switch.

6. Summary of the chapter

In this chapter, we have given the theoretical design of a QTTH network and estimated the potential of using the commercially available equipment to generate the secret quantum keys.

Our initial evaluations have shown that the CV-QKD protocol has the potential to be used at access network level and up to 100 Mbits/s SKR can be attained for back-to-back transmissions. While for FTTH networks, 25 Mbits/s SKR can be achieved for T = 0.8, that is, equivalent 10 km of the optical fiber transmission. These key rates are much higher than the commercially available encrypters based on DV-protocol. The CV-QKD protocol is compatible with network components like multiplexers and demultiplexers. Due to this benefit, we can multiplex several quantum signals together to transfer aggregate high SKR in the range of 1 Gbit/s. Moreover, the splitting ratio associated with the commercially available optical passive splitters influence the SKR and dramatically abase beyond 1 × 8 splitting ratio. These results provide a solid base to enhance the existing telecommunication infrastructure and modules to deliver end-to-end optical data encryption to the subscribers.

Acknowledgements

The work is supported by School of Computing, Edinburgh Napier University (ENU) Internal Research Grants for the project STRENGTH (Scalable, Tunable, Resilient and Encrypted Next Generation Transmission Hub (grant no. 830965). Special thanks to: (a) Prof. Alan Woodward from University of Surrey, UK for his valuable inputs and discussions on the future of QKD networks and (b) Dr. M. A. Haithem from Case Western Reserve University, Ohio USA for providing us with the valuable data on MEMS and QKD.

Conflict of interest

The authors declare that there is no conflict of interest regarding the publication of this book chapter.

Author details

Rameez Asif[1,2]* and William J. Buchanan[1,2]

*Address all correspondence to: r.asif@napier.ac.uk

1 Centre for Distributed Computing, Networks, and Security, School of Computing, Edinburgh Napier University, Edinburgh, UK

2 The Cyber Academy, Edinburgh Napier University, UK

References

[1] Asif R. Advanced and flexible multi-carrier receiver architecture for high-count multi-core fiber based space division multiplexed applications. Scientific Reports. 2016;**6**:27465

[2] Ding Y, Kamchevska V, Dalgaard K, et al. Reconfigurable SDM switching using novel silicon photonic integrated circuit. Scientific Reports. 2016;**6**:39058

[3] Lam CF, Liu H, Koley B, et al. Fiber optic communication technologies: What's needed for data center network operation? IEEE Communications Magazine. 2010;**48**(7):32-39

[4] Lam CF. Fiber to the home: Getting beyond 10 Gigabit/sec. Optics & Photonics News. 2016;**27**(3):22-29

[5] Horstmeyer R, Judkewitz B, Vellekoop IM, et al. Physical key-protected one-time pad. Scientific Reports. 2013;**3**:3543

[6] Gisin N, Ribordy G, Tittel W, et al. Quantum cryptography. Reviews of Modern Physics. 2002;**74**:145-195

[7] Lo HK, Curty M, Tamaki K. Secure quantum key distribution. Nature Photonics. 2014;**8**: 595-604

[8] Wootters W, Zurek W. A single quantum cannot be cloned. Nature. 1982;**299**:802-803

[9] Korzh B, Ci Wen Lim C, Gisin HNR, et al. Provably secure and practical quantum key distribution over 307km of optical fibre. Nature Photonics. 2014;**9**:163-168

[10] Frolich B, Dynes J, Lucamarini M, et al. Quantum secured gigabit optical access networks. Scientific Reports. 2015;**5**:18121(1)-18121(7)

[11] Comandar L, Lucamarini M, Frolich B, et al. Quantum key distribution without detector vulnerabilities using optically seeded lasers. Nature Photonics. 2016;**10**:312-315

[12] Ma X, Qi B, Zhao Y, et al. Practical decoy state for quantum key distribution. Physical Review A. 2005;**72**:012326

[13] Zhao Y, Qi B, Ma X, et al. Experimental quantum key distribution with decoy states. Physical Review Letters. 2006;**96**:070502

[14] Soh DBS, Brif C, Coles PJ, et al. Self-referenced continuous-variable quantum key distribution protocol. Physical Review X. 2015;**5**:041010

[15] Jouguet P, Kunz-Jacques S, Leverrier A, et al. Experimental demonstration of long distance continuous-variable quantum key distribution. Nature Photonics. 2013;**7**:378-381

[16] Huang D, Huang P, Li H, et al. Field demonstration of a continuous-variable quantum key distribution network. Optics Letters. 2016;**41**(15):3511-3514

[17] Stucki D, Barreiro C, Fasel S, et al. Continuous high speed coherent one-way quantum key distribution. Optics Express. 2009;**17**(16):13326-13334

[18] Qi B, Huang LL, Qian L, et al. Experimental study on the gaussian-modulated coherent state quantum key distribution over standard telecommunication fibers. Physical Review A. 2007;**76**:052323

[19] Derkach I, Usenko VC, Filip R. Preventing side-channel effects in continuous-variable quantum key distribution. Physical Review A. 2016;**93**:032309

[20] Painchaud Y, Poulin M, Morin M, et al. Performance of balanced detection in a coherent receiver. Optics Express. 2009;**17**(5):3659-3672

[21] Leverrier A, Allffeaume R, Boutros J, et al. Multidimensional reconciliation for a continuous-variable quantum key distribution. Physical Review A. 2008;**77**:042325

[22] Chi YM, Qi B, Zhu W, et al. A balanced homodyne detector for high-rate gaussian modulated coherent-state quantum key distribution. New Journal of Physics. 2011;**13**(1): 013003

[23] Asif R, Buchanan W. Seamless cryptographic key generation via off-the-shelf telecommunication components for end-to-end data encryption. In: 10th IEEE International Conference on Internet of Things (iThings-2017), Exeter, UK: 2017. paper ID: SITN-2

[24] Lin CY, Asif R, Holtmannspoetter M, et al. Nonlinear mitigation using carrier phase estimation and digital backward propagation in coherent QAM transmission. Optics Express. 2012;**20**(26):B405-B412

[25] Qu Z, Djordjevic IB, Neifeld MA. Rf-subcarrier-assisted four-state continuous-variable QKD based on coherent detection. Optics Letters. 2016;**41**(23):5507-5510

[26] Karlsson A, Bourennane M, Ribordy G, et al. A single-photon counter for long-haul telecom. IEEE Circuits and Devices Magazine. 1999;**15**(6):34-40

[27] Comandar LC, Frauhlich B, Lucamarini M, et al. Room temperature single-photon detectors for high bit rate quantum key distribution. Applied Physics Letters. 2014;**104**(2): 021101

[28] Froehlich B, Lucamarini M, Dynes JF, et al. Long-distance quantum key distribution secure against coherent attacks. Optica. 2017;**4**(1):163-167

[29] Asif R, Ye F, Morioka T. Lambda-Selection Strategy in C+L band 1-pbit/s (448 wdm/19-core/ 128 gbit/s/channel) Ex-grid Space Division Multiplexed Transmission. Paris, France: European Conference on Networking and Communication (EUCNC); 2015. pp. 321-324

[30] Razavi M. Multiple-access quantum key distribution networks. IEEE Transactions on Communications. 2012;**60**(10):3071-3079

[31] Bahrani S, Razavi M, Salehi JA. Optimal Wavelength Allocation in Hybrid Quantum Classical Networks. arXiv: 2018. pp. 483-487.1701.08270

[32] Fossier S, Diamanti E, Debuisschert T, et al. Field test of a continuous-variable quantum key distribution prototype. New Journal of Physics. 2009;**11**(4):045023

[33] Huang D, Lin D, Wang C, et al. Continuous-variable quantum key distribution with 1-megabit per second secure key rate. Optics Express. 2015;**23**(13):17511-17519

Chapter 3

Software Quality Assurance

Kazu Okumoto, Rashid Mijumbi and
Abhaya Asthana

Additional information is available at the end of the chapter

http://dx.doi.org/10.5772/intechopen.79839

Abstract

Telecom networks are composed of very complex software-controlled systems. In recent years, business and technology needs are pushing vendors towards service agility where they must continuously develop, deliver, and improve such software over very short cycles. Moreover, being critical infrastructure, Telecom systems must meet important operational, legal, and regulatory requirements in terms of quality and performance to avoid outages. To ensure high quality software, processes and models must be put in place to enable quick and easy decision making across the development cycle. In this chapter, we will discuss the background and recent trends in software quality assurance. We will then introduce BRACE: a cloud-based, fully-automated tool for software defect prediction, reliability and availability modeling and analytics. In particular, we will discuss a novel Software Reliability Growth Modeling (SRGM) algorithm that is the core of BRACE. The algorithm provides defect prediction for both early and late stages of the software development cycle. To illustrate and validate the tool and algorithm, we also discuss key use cases, including actual defect and outage data from two large-scale software development projects from telecom products. BRACE is being successfully used by global teams of various large-scale software development projects.

Keywords: software quality & reliability assurance, telecommunication software, software defect measurements & modeling

1. Introduction

Emerging technology breakthroughs in a number of fields, such The Internet of Things, 5G, artificial intelligence, etc., are propelling a continuous increase in the size and complexity of software in communication systems. In such applications, software must have—among others—two important characteristics: (1) quality and (2) agility. Software quality is important to limit downtime and vulnerabilities that might have unprecedented consequences for the anticipated societal-critical applications, while agility helps to continuously improve services to meet customer needs. In order to meet business objectives, and supported by advances in virtualization technologies, Telecom service providers are recently moving towards service agility, where the aim is to create new or improve the services provided to their users [1]. To this end, network software vendors must have the capability to continuously deliver and integrate software from which such services are composed.

These requirements mean that development teams must be able to produce quality software in very short time periods. This calls for accurate ways of planning team resource requirements or software size (number/complexity of features) ahead of time to avoid failing to meet customer needs. A useful approach for this assessment is *predicting the number of defects* during the requirements and design phase, which may allow for time to take preventive actions such as additional reviews and more extensive testing, finally improving software process control and achieving high software quality [2].

1.1. Software development phases

Software quality can be significantly affected by the number of defects and amount/type of testing carried out at the different stages of the software development phase. In this subsection, we examine the defect flow through various development phases and in the field. Once a set of new features is identified, each of them goes through the phases shown in **Figure 1**. It can be observed that there are a number of activities overlapping in time (*x-axis*). New defects are introduced during the requirement, design and coding phases while old defects are carried over from previous releases into the current release. The thickness of the arrows indicates the relative numbers of defects expected at each point in time. Defects are found and removed or

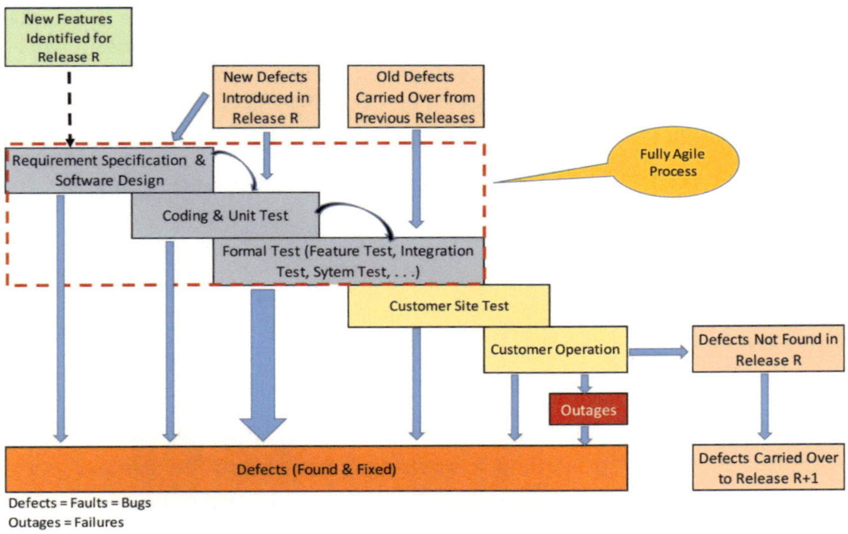

Figure 1. Defect flow development, test, field (traditional vs. agile).

fixed during every development phase as well as during customer site test and actual operation periods. In a traditional development process, most defects are found by testers, independent of developers. The test phase includes integration, feature, system, robustness, stability, and performance testing, just to name a few.[1] Most software defects are expected to be found and removed during these testing phases.

A proportion of defects that remain at the end of the test phase are normally encountered during operation in the field, and usually, only a fraction of them lead to failures or outages. However, an outage puts a system down, making it go through a process of respond-recover-resolve. Finally, some of the residual defects will usually not be found even during field operation. These then become base or old defects for the following release.

1.2. SRGM background

The quality of software is measured in terms of software defects found during the customer operation period. SRGM is usually used to quantify the quality of software products before they are delivered to customers. SRGM is a very well-studied subject, with over 200 SRGMs developed since early 1970s [3–15]. These models can generally be categorized as either being *parametric* or *non-parametric*.

Parametric models are based on explicit mathematical expressions and physical interpretation. They were originally designed for system test but continue to be extended to include functional, integration, and other earlier test phases. They are the earliest developed models, are easily understood, and widely used. Most of the frequently used parametric models can be systematically grouped based on the shape of the function (i.e. *S-shaped* curve or *exponential* curve). S-shaped curve models use various types of S-shaped distributions such as Gamma, logistic, Weibull functions to match with actual data trends [6, 9], while exponential models (e.g. [3, 4, 7, 10, 11]) consider that defects are found at a constant rate through the different test phases. S-curve models have flexibility in describing different shapes of the trend since they have more than two parameters. Compared with S-shaped models, exponential models are simple with only two parameters and have been successfully demonstrated with practical data from large-scale software development projects [16, 17]. There have been many comparison studies performed and various tools have been developed for evaluating individual models in terms of how well each model fits to the data [18, 19].

Recently, non-parametric SRGMs are being proposed. Such models typically use *machine learning* techniques considering the inherent characteristics of the software (such as code size, test resources, test duration, complexity, etc.) as input. Although non-parametric models are promising, their use in practical applications is still limited by their need for (big amounts of) input data which is not always available, or whose quality may be unacceptable. Therefore, practical implementations and application of SRGMs are still mainly based on parametric models. Even then, there is no single model which can be used in every situation [20]. Models that work well during the early development phases are typically not efficient in the later

[1]It is worth noting that test phase names vary across projects and organizations.

stages, in which case a complete solution may require more than one model. In addition, the fact that the rate at which defects are found can change overtime requires that even for the same phase, the same model may need to be applied more than once each covering a specific trend. In practice, applying such models in an efficient way can be effort intensive and usually requires an expert.

This chapter discusses advances to the above techniques and approaches using BRACE [21], a cloud-based, fully-automated tool for software defect prediction, reliability and availability modeling and analytics. BRACE includes a number of technical contributions to make software defect prediction more practical for every software development project. First, the tool unifies and automates the entire process of data extraction, pre-processing, core processing and post-processing. Second, the core data analytics engine of BRACE—SRGM—provides a robust, consistent, flexible, fast, statistically sound approach to defect prediction for any defect data set without human intervention. This is achieved by modeling the entire defect trend as a series of piece-wise exponential curves, and incorporating a mechanism to automatically detect when to transition from one curve to the next. Moreover, to enhance the accuracy, whenever available, the algorithm can also take as input feature arrival data (which is a measure of development effort). This allows the enhanced SRGM to provide defect prediction from the project planning phase through the internal testing phase and the customer site test and customer operation periods. Finally, BRACE exposes a user interface which displays the output generated from the core processing. It makes it easier for projects to understand the current progress towards quality improvement. To the best of our knowledge, this is the first attempt to propose a practical software defect prediction and reliability management solution that can be re-used across multiple teams at industrial scale.

1.3. Chapter overview

The rest of this chapter is organized as follows: In Section 2, we present the design, implementation and use cases of BRACE. We also describe datasets from two example projects that are used as references throughout the chapter. In Section 3, we detail an automated SRGM algorithm which is the core analytics engine of BRACE. The algorithm enhances traditional SRGMs by enabling accurate early defect prediction, which, as mentioned earlier, is a necessity for most projects. Sections 4 and 5 will discuss key post-delivery metrics: *customer defects* and *software availability* respectively. The Chapter is concluded in Section 5. Data sets from two large-scale software development projects from telecom products are used to illustrate the effectiveness of BRACE throughout the chapter.

2. BRACE system overview

2.1. System design

BRACE consists of three main processes: (1) *pre-processing*, (2) *core processing* and (3) *post-processing* as illustrated in **Figure 2**.

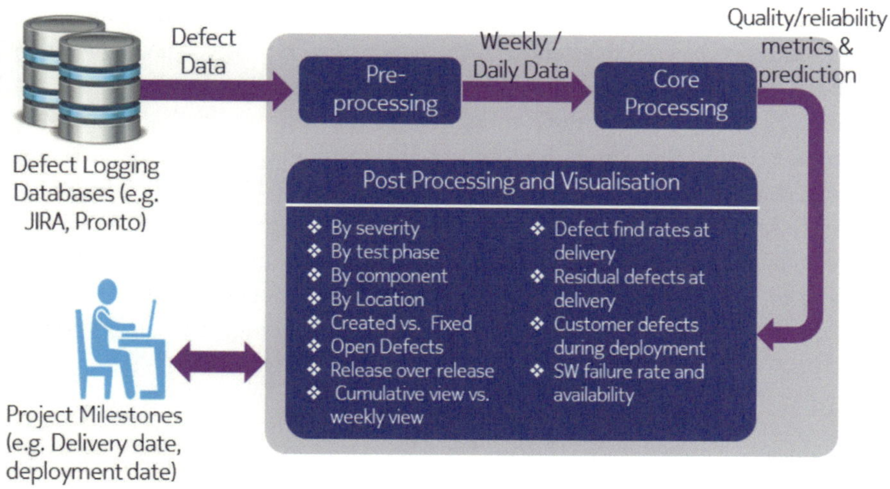

Figure 2. BRACE main processes.

1. The pre-processing step is made up of a generic data-collector which uses application programming interfaces (APIs) to collect data from various sources. As example, defect data can be obtained from Jira while other project-related information may be obtained from GitLab. The data is generally obtained as records of defects with the corresponding fields (such as creation date, resolution date, defect type, software release, etc.). Once the data is received for project, a number of processing steps are carried out. These might include—as necessary—*filtering* out specific defects based on any chosen field, *mapping* particular field/values, *grouping* defects based on any of the fields, etc. These processing steps may be generic for all projects, or may also be customized for a particular project. The output of this step is defect numbers aggregated over time (for example defects each day, 3-days, week[2]) for any desired *profile*. The *profiles* are project-specific analysis groupings such as defects related to a given software component, development location, severity, etc.

2. The core processing implements the optimization function which derives *maximum likelihood* estimates of the model parameters for a given set of defect data. It then—dynamically and automatically—identifies changes in the defect trend as new defect data is added. This is achieved by comparing the goodness-of-fit of the predicted values to actual data points. It eventually generates multiple curves to describe the entire defect trend using a piece-wise application of NHPP exponential models. The last curve is used for predicting total defects and residual defects at delivery. Detailed discussions on the SRGM used by the core processing step are presented in Section 3.

[2]While defect trend analysis is typically performed with weekly data, as we move towards continuous delivery, it is necessary to investigate the use of daily data. Therefore, the proposed tool has been applied to daily defect data from several projects, and has been able to produce results consistent with those from weekly data. Allowing the use of daily data is important as this allows SRGM to be applied in real time (daily), and hence help detect possible problems earlier.

3. Finally, the post-processing step takes as input the metrics from the core processing so as to generate various types of tables and charts, depending on project's needs. As an example, this step may be able to present outputs such as software failure rate, software availability & reliability, software annual downtime, defect rate, and predicted defects. Moreover, it also provides confidence limits for each of the calculated metrics. Therefore, the post-processing stage is aimed at providing answers (using a GUI) to the questions presented in **Table 1**. Answers to these use cases are the main motivations of the work done by software reliability experts, and by extension the main motivations of BRACE. As such, answers to the questions below will be provided throughout the rest of this chapter. We discuss details regarding these outputs and final processing steps in Sections 4 and 5, respectively.

2.2. Defect data sets

Defect data sets, called Projects A & B, are briefly described. Both projects represent large-scale software development from telecom products. **Figure 3** shows an example of a 3G & 4G wireless network system, where projects A and B can be found in the diagram.

2.2.1. Project A

This is a key wireless product, called RNC, which is responsible for the control and management of radio resources in a wireless network. It is a large-scale software development for a key 3G wireless telecommunication product with a high availability redundant hardware configuration. Code size varies from over 500 KNCSL (1000 non-commentary source lines) in earlier releases to less than 100 KNCSL as customers migrate from 3G to 4G systems. A traditional delivery scheme of one delivery per release was used. A major hardware platform change took place during the reported period, which resulted in redesigning the software architecture.

It takes advantages of hardware technological improvement, by introducing additional software redundancy as well as upgrading and re-designing the hardware platform with a pair of active-active processors. The new hardware platform supports multiple copies of a key

1.	How many defects are we going to find by delivery date?
2.	How many residual defects will remain at delivery?
3.	Are we ready for delivery?
4.	When do we expect the defect closure curve to catch up with the defect arrival curve?
5.	How many defects are we going to find after delivery?
6.	How does the defect curve of a new release compare to past releases?
7.	Which location/severity/component is generating the most defects?
8.	Can we combine inherent defects from previous releases, defects found within the current release and defects deferred to next release?
9.	Are we finding defects as expected?
10.	Can we adjust for DevOps continuous integration & delivery (CI/CD)?
11.	Can we predict software availability?

Table 1. BRACE use cases (motivating questions).

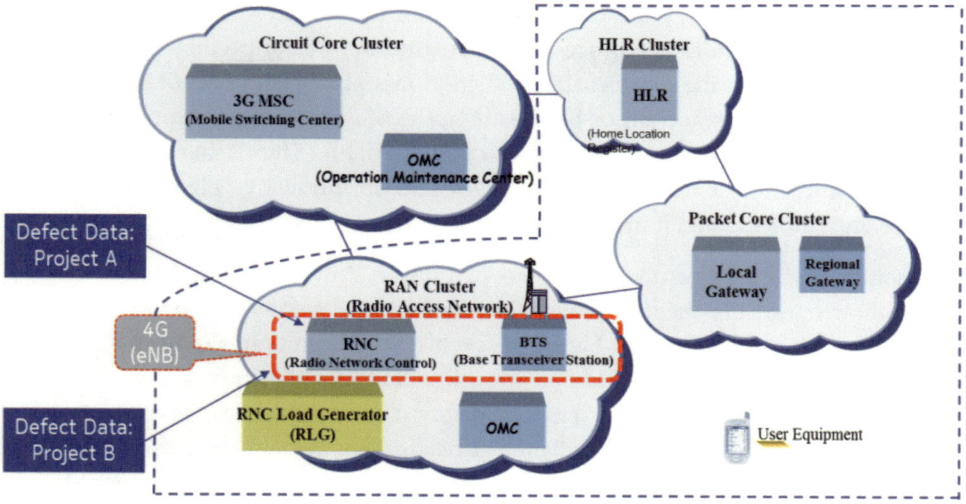

Figure 3. Sample 3G & 4G wireless telecom network system.

software component as many pairs of active-standby software configurations. As discussed in Section 4, this feature helped improve the capacity as well as the availability since the impact of failure software becomes very small due to a pair of active-standby. The quality impact of the major changes will be highlighted in Section 4. The data sets used in this chapter cover 11 releases over 5 years.

2.2.2. Project B

It represents a radio access part of the latest 4G mobile network technology. The two 3G key functions were combined into one, called eNB, to meet high data rate requirements. It performs the control and management of radio resources in a wireless network, plus radio frequency transmitters and receivers used to directly communicate with mobile devices. It is built on a highly complex hardware design and sophisticated software architecture. The software development is required to deliver many complex new features to meet demand in fast growing markets. Recent releases contain over 1 million non-commentary source lines (MNCSL) new features and deploy a new delivery scheme of multiple deliveries per release to satisfy the needs for additional features by multiple customers. Similar to Project A, this project also went through a major hardware platform change and drastic software redesign. The quality impact will be shown in Section 4.

3. Software reliability growth model (SRGM)

3.1. Automated SRGM

As earlier mentioned, exponential models assume that defects can be found and resolved at a constant rate [10]. While this results into a simple and flexible model with well understood assumptions, it is not always the case that software development is stable, as sometimes changes have to be made to the processes. To ensure that defect prediction adapts to such trend changes, we apply the exponential prediction model to each wave of software defects. The idea of piecewise application of SRGMs is not exactly new. For example, a concept for evolving software content was originally discussed in [10]. This is the first time that we successfully formulated it mathematically, developed an innovative algorithm to automate the process and implemented it in a cloud environment.

The mathematical model is a non-homogeneous Poisson Process (NHPP) with a mean value function following an exponential model. The tool uses a piece-wise application of NHPP exponential models as illustrated in **Figure 4**. The NHPP assumption is used to implement the statistical method of maximum likelihood for estimating model parameters with the normal approximation confidence limits for a set of defect data. As new test defect data becomes available, we continuously monitor and predict residual (or remaining) defects at delivery. It then uses the last curve for predicting defects to be found after delivery to customer site.

To illustrate the model, consider a finite number, a, of defects such that each defect is found and removed by time, t, following a cumulative distribution function, $F(t)$. For a defect find process, $N(t)$, the probability of finding n defects by time t is in general expressed as a binomial distribution given in (1).

$$P\{N(t) = n\} = \binom{a}{n} F(t)^n [1 - F(t)]^{a-n} \tag{1}$$

In practice, the value of a is large, and therefore we can approximate (1) by a Poisson distribution with the mean value function, $m(t)$, as given in (2).

$$P\{N(t) = n\} = m(t)^n \exp\{-m(t)\}/n! \tag{2}$$

Note that $m(t) = aF(t)$ represents the average number of defects found by time t. An exponential model is described as an NHPP with the mean value function:

$$m(t) = a\{1 - \exp(-bt)\} \tag{3}$$

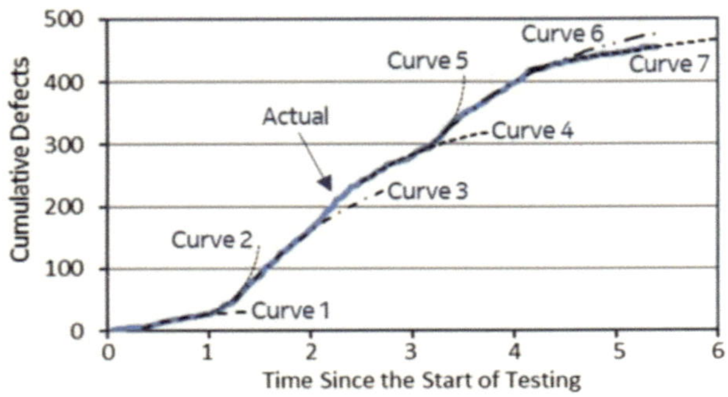

Figure 4. An example of a piece-wise application of NHPP model.

The parameters *a* and *b* represent total defects in the software and the rate at which each defect is found, respectively. Therefore, a total of *a* defects is assumed to be found according to an exponential distribution with a rate of *b*. Note that the parameter *a* represents the number of defects associated with each period for a case of piece-wise application. Since the mean value function is a function of time, it is called an exponential NHPP model. Taking the derivative of the mean value function we can derive the corresponding defect intensity function or defect rate, given in (4):

$$\lambda(t) = ab\exp(-bt) \tag{4}$$

It should be pointed out that if *b* is positive, m(t) converges exponentially, approaching to a positive value of *a*, and λ(t) decreases exponentially. This is a typical trend for reliability growth. As *b* approaches zero and *a* tends to infinity, $m(t)$ becomes a straight line and $\lambda(t)$ becomes constant, i.e., a stationary Poisson process. If both *a* and *b* are negative, both $m(t)$ and $\lambda(t)$ increase exponentially. Although most of the time *b* is positive, there are a few cases with *b* tending to zero during site test and in-service periods and *b* being negative in early test phases. Note that the basic assumption of a finite number of defects is violated if *b* is zero or negative. However, it will be useful in explaining different trends for individual test periods within the same release. We will discuss further with actual data later.

Answers to use cases (a), (b) & (c) in Section 2 can be illustrated using **Figure 5** as follows: SRGM predicts 3700 defects by the delivery date. Therefore, assuming that current date corresponds to week 19 (vertical blue line), we would expect to find 1200 more defects in the 11 weeks to delivery assuming the same test progress continues. Since SRGM predicts a total of 4500 defects and 3700 defects at delivery, the *residual defects* will be 800 (= 4500–3700). The percentage residual defect can be calculated as 18% (= 800 / 4500). Based on our experience, we have determined thresholds (the percentage of residual defects to total defects) and provide color codes that are indicative of software quality and the readiness to deliver. Specifically,

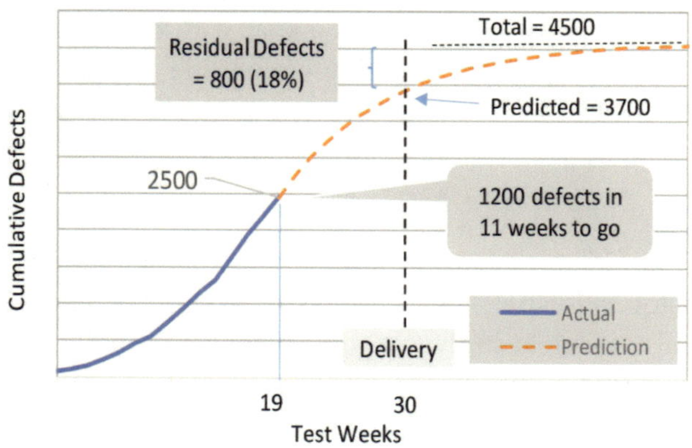

Figure 5. Example of software defect prediction.

readiness is given as green (implying 'good to go') if the threshold is less than 15%, yellow if it is between 15% and 25%, and red if it is greater than 25%. In this example, the software falls in the yellow range, indicating that some caution is needed if the project decides to proceed with the planned delivery.

As illustrated above, residual defects, which are derived from the defect arrival curve using SRGM, play a key role in software quality assessment in terms of delivery readiness. Our recommendation is that readiness is given as green (implying 'good to go') if the threshold is less than 15%, yellow if it is between 15 and 25%, and red if it is greater than 25%. In addition, it is important to track backlog defects at delivery, so as not to deliver known issues. Our recommendation is that all customer critical and major issues be resolved by delivery. We will address how to predict backlog defects in Section 3.2.2.

3.2. Enhanced SRGM: early defect prediction model (eDPM)

Typical SRGM techniques require defect data from the software test period. This limits their use during the early phases of software development during which it is usually necessary to make important (and time intensive) decisions (such as the level of staffing or amount of required testing or number of features to focus on) about the development process. Considering the industry trend towards very short software development lifecycles (i.e. agile development), it is essential to be able to make such decisions accurately very early on in the development phase. Specifically, in order to determine the staffing requirements for development and test activities during the early planning phase, many projects now need to understand what the defect find curve would look like during the internal test period. Therefore, early software defect prediction is needed for the early identification of software quality, cost overrun, and optimal development strategy.

We propose a novel method, eDPM, for predicting defect arrival curves based on the feature arrival curve during the planning phase. The feature arrival curve often gives the number of sub-features for each feature of the project, together with the times when each sub-feature is expected to be completed. Such information is usually available during the development planning phase of the software development life cycle. Specifically, eDPM involves using data from a previous release of the same product, together with the feature arrival curve for the upcoming release. In order to produce a reliability modeling approach that covers the whole development process, the eDPM approach has been integrated into BRACE as an enhanced SRGM.

3.2.1. Transformation functions

eDPM uses two transformation functions: one horizontal shift and one vertical shift. We have performed a statistical correlation study (e.g., quantile-quantile or Q-Q plot [22]) and found a very high correlation. **Figure 6** illustrates a Q-Q plot for Project B data. If the data points follow a straight line, it indicates a strong correlation between two factors being considered or statistically, the distributions of the two factors are the same. That is, both curves have similarity in shape.

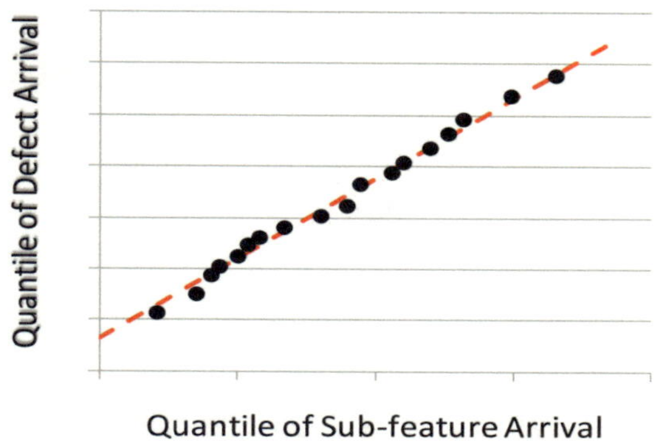

Figure 6. A sample Q-Q plot for project B release 5 data.

Let (x, y) represent a feature curve and (x_{new}, y_{new}) represent a defect arrival curve. We can move the feature curve to the right and closer to the defect arrival curve with the horizontal shift function in (5)

$$x_{new} = \alpha + \beta x \tag{5}$$

where α and β are parameters intrinsic to an individual release. The parameter α represents the average time to find α defects, and β represents the additional delay in the defect find process, likely due to a test resource constraint or critical bugs. Next, we use a simple form for the vertical shift as shown in (6).

$$y_{new} = \gamma y \tag{6}$$

The parameter γ is determined as a ratio of the feature count and the defect count used for the best fitted line in the Q-Q plot. It represents the number of defects per feature. Combining (5) and (6), we can transform the feature curve to represent the defect arrival curve. If previous release data is not available, we can use defect data from the initial test period. **Figure 7** demonstrates that feature ready curve is a good leading indicator for defect arrival curves. The feature arrival data is readily available for most projects.

3.2.2. Case studies

We will now provide four case studies to demonstrate the robustness of eDPM for practical uses. It should be pointed out that the team "feature" is used here in a generic sense to represent either sub-feature, epic, story, or sprint depending on the availability of metrics for individual projects. Similarly, the term "release" represents a set of features defined for each software delivery. The release content continues to evolve over the software lifecycle. It is important to continuously monitor the release content and adjust the transformation functions to improve the prediction accuracy. While out of scope for this chapter, we have recently developed an algorithm which automates the estimation of parameters as new feature and defect data becomes available.

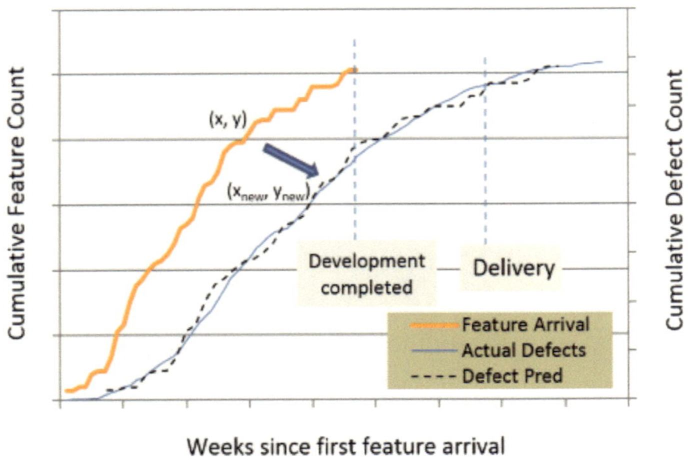

Figure 7. eDPM defect arrival curve prediction based on feature arrival curve.

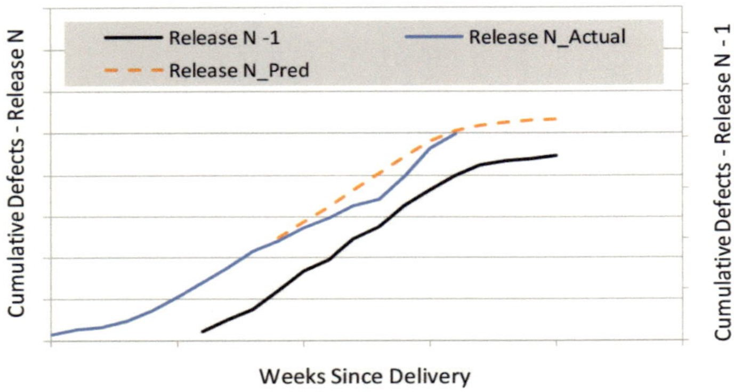

Figure 8. eDPM case study #1: Previous release data.

Case Study #1—Previous release data: This case study considers a project without feature ready data available. We use previous release data, called Release N – 1, to predict the defect arrival curve for Release N. Using the transformation functions described in Section 3.2.1 and the test defect data from Release N, we can predict the defect arrival curve, as shown in **Figure 8**. Actual data is overlaid and compared against the predicted arrival curve. The several weeks (between −10 and −5) the actual data was not following the predicted curve were due to a few critical issues slowing down the test progress. Once they were cleared with fixes, the test progress was quickly recovered and the defects started to come in as expected.

Case Study #2—Test cases executed: This case considers a project without accurate data on feature ready dates, but having a good record of test cases executed prior to handing the features over to the test team. For our eDPM purpose the test case data is considered equivalent to the feature ready data. **Figure 9** demonstrates near-perfect prediction of the defect arrival curve using test cases executed.

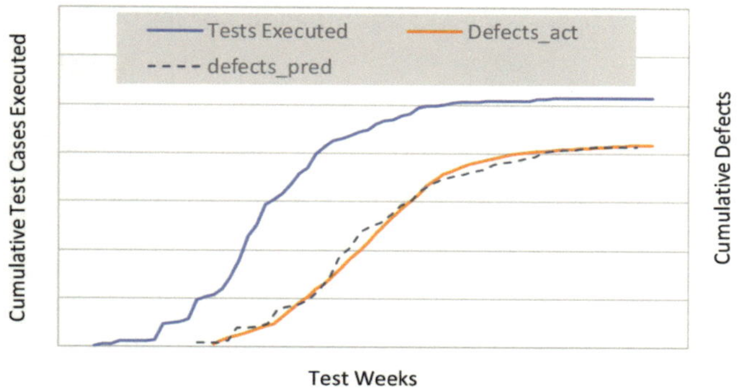

Figure 9. eDMP case study #2: Test cases executed vs. test defects.

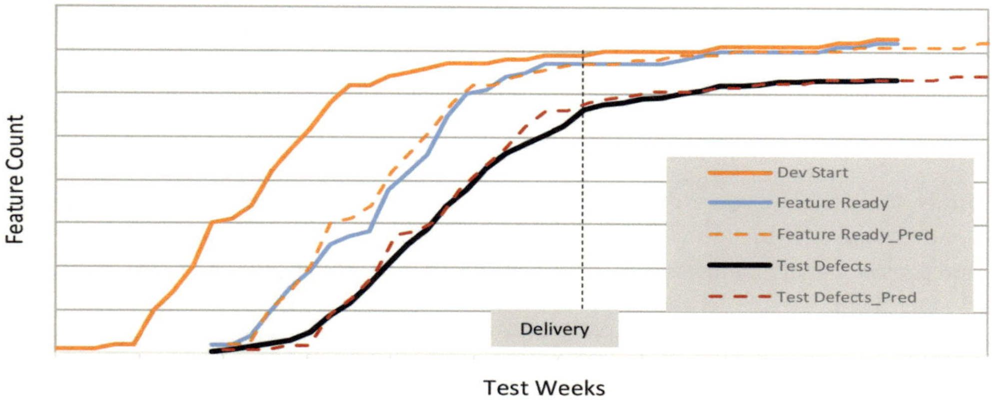

Figure 10. eDPM case study #3: Development start vs. feature ready vs. test defects.

Case Study #3—Feature development start data: This considers a project with a good record of feature development status. We first use feature ready dates to predict the defect arrival curve. As expected, it gives a good prediction. The next task is to evaluate if we can use the development start dates to predict the feature ready curve and the defect arrival curve. This is important to help a project to plan the development and test resources for both feature ready dates and test defects. In this case we apply the transformation functions in two phases, i.e., one for predicting feature ready curve and the other for predicting the defect arrival curve. As illustrated in **Figure 10**, the predictions are remarkably accurate for both cases.

Case Study #4—DevOps CI/CD story points completed: The case considers a DevOps continuous integration & delivery project with a delivery interval of 2 or 3 weeks. The project implements a full Agile development process. **Figure 11** shows cumulative views of story points and integration test defects in two different vertical scales. The vertical lines represent individual release dates. A user story is a very low-level definition of a requirement, containing just enough information so that the developers can produce a reasonable estimate of the effort to implement it. A story point is a measure of the effort required to implement a story. It is a relative measure of complexity, albeit a subjective one. However, if it is done in a consistent manner, it can be used as a good leading indicator for predicting defects, as shown in **Figure 11**.

It was later confirmed that there were two major process changes made during the reported period. As eDPM was applied to the data (Transformation #1), we were able to identify the trend change after several months where the transformation is no longer valid. It turns out that the trend change occurred when a major process change was made. Another set of transformation functions, called Transformation #2, were then used. The predicted values are very closely matching with actual defect data. Several months later, we encountered another trend change, which turns out to be caused by another major process change. We then used another transformation #3. With the successive use of eDPM we demonstrated that defects can be predicted with reasonable accuracy for the entire reported period.

Another benefit of eDPM is to help quantify the process improvement. One of the parameters, γ, as described in Eq. (6), represents defects per story point in this case study. By comparing the values of γ between two transformation periods, we can calculate the relative change in γ values. This relative change represents the percent of improvement due to the process change. To further provide the significance of this benefit, we were able to quantify an improvement of 10 and 70% for the first process change and the second, respectively.

Case Study #5—Defect closure data: This case study we consider a project with both defect arrival and closure data in addition to sub-feature arrival data. This project is still in early test phase but project management wants to know whether the defect backlog can reach zero at the delivery date. First, we predict the defect arrival curve based on the sub-feature arrival data and actual defect arrival data so far using eDPM. We then predict the closure curve based on the predicted arrival curve using eDPM. By combining the predicted arrival and closure curves we can now calculate the defect backlog by subtracting the closure curve from the arrival curve. **Figure 12** shows the predicted arrival and closure curves, along with the predicted defect backlog curve. The project can now see some actions to be taken to improve the backlog curve to get closer to zero at the delivery date.

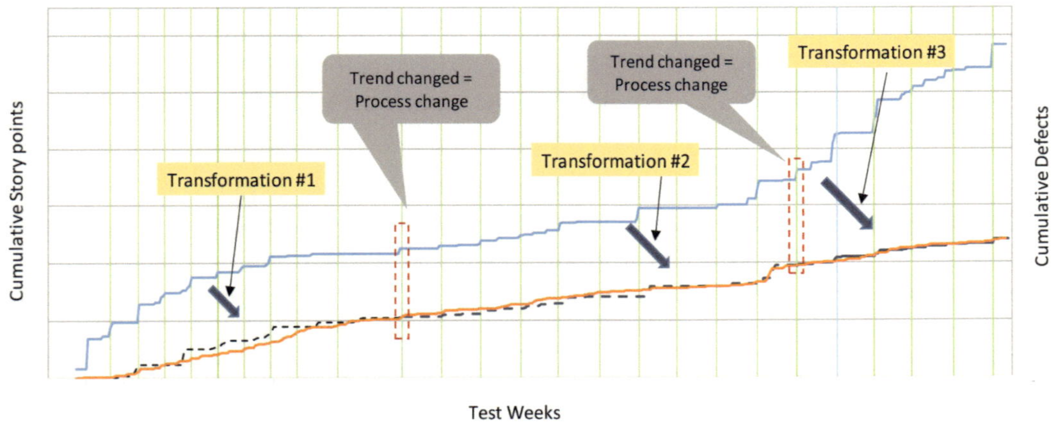

Figure 11. eDPM case study #4: Story points vs. integration test defects.

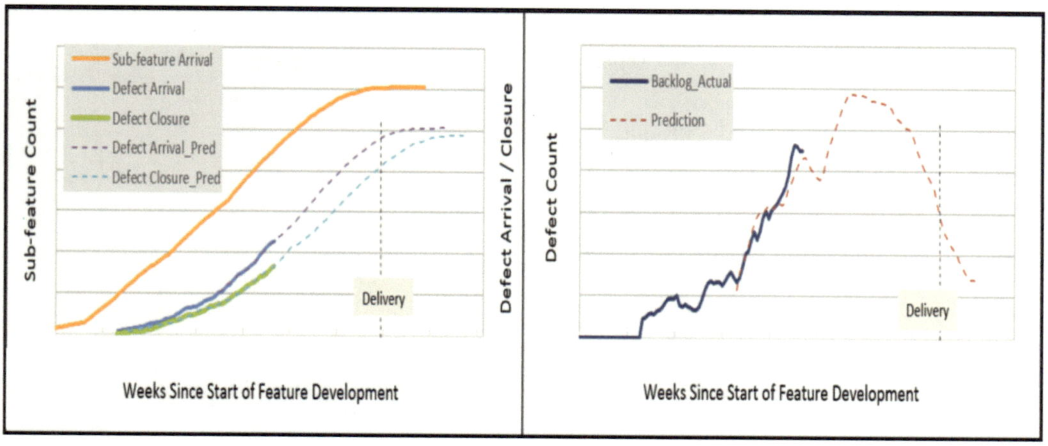

Figure 12. eDPM case study #5: sub-feature, defect arrival/closure/backlog.

4. Customer defect prediction

In Section 3, we demonstrated that the last curve prior to software delivery represents the final product from which the total number of defects and residual defects can be calculated. Previous release data or historical data from other projects will be helpful for determining the percent of delivered defects to be found during the operation period. See [16] for detailed discussions.

The assumption that the defect curve can be extended from the development phase into the operational phase (e.g. [23–25]) does not hold in practice, as there are usually discontinuities due to changes in the intensity of testing, as well as operational conditions not always being exactly the same as test environments [7].

To highlight the procedure and results we will use defect data taken from Project B. **Figure 13** shows a cumulative view of customer defect prediction. Note that the curve should be always above the actual data after delivery. The difference between the curve and the last actual data

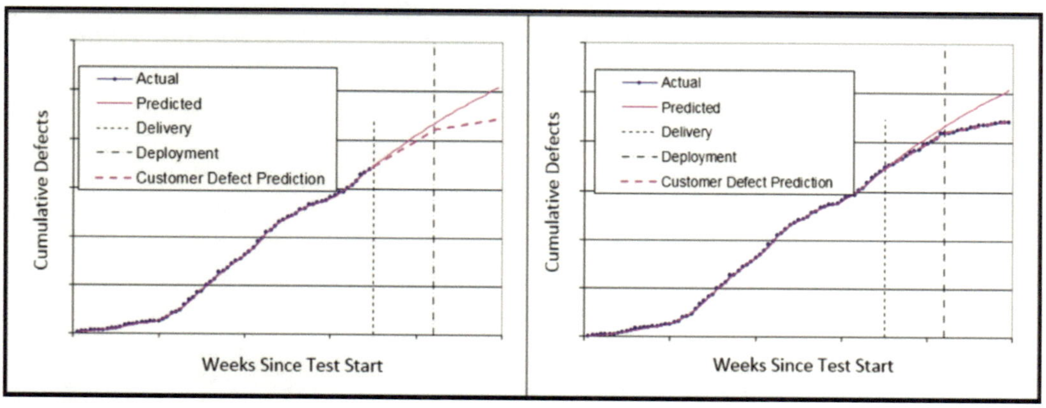

Figure 13. Cumulative view of project B customer defect prediction vs. actual.

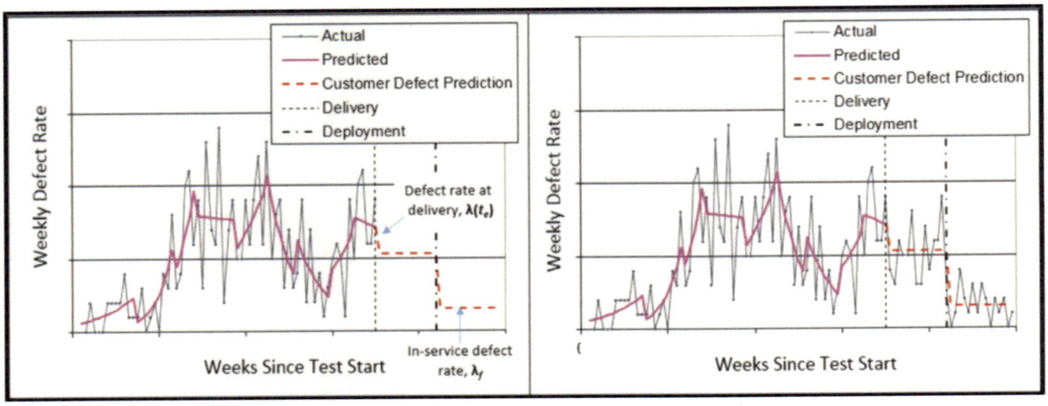

Figure 14. Weekly view of project B customer defect prediction vs. actual.

point indicates the defects not found in this release and they will become a part of the next release. That is, not all delivered defects will be found during the operation period. It also demonstrates that actual data follows as predicted, indicating the importance of historical data in predicting post-delivery defects.

Figure 14 illustrates the difference in defect rate, $\lambda(t_e)$, at the end of test phase, t_e, and during the operation period, λ_f. It can be observed that there is a difference in defect rate, likely due to differences in the intensity of testing during the two periods, as well as possible differences between a test environment and a field operational state.

5. Software failure rate, availability, and reliability

In recent years many product suppliers have been implementing complex software-controlled systems with a large number of software features on a short development schedule. In the telecom industry, a critical customer operational issue is on system performance, especially in terms of system outages impacting the service availability for their end users. As a result, service providers frequently ask their product suppliers for software reliability and availability measurements. In this section, we discuss the relationship between software failure rate, availability, and reliability.

5.1. Software failure rate

Field outage measurements are required for telecom products by TL9000 [26], which is a quality management system (QMS). It standardizes the quality system requirements for the design, development, delivery, installation, and maintenance of telecom products and services. It defines the reliability in terms of SO3 (service outage frequency) and SO4 (service outage duration) metrics. As demonstrated in [16] the defect find process during the operation period maybe modeled as a stationary Poisson process. It also follows that the rate of software failure (or outage) rate for each release can be modeled as stationary Poisson process. Consider a software release with a failure rate λ and defect rate λ_f. It is worth noting that λ is usually measured in terms of failures per year. The defect conversion factor may be expressed as shown in Eq. (7)

$$d = \frac{\lambda}{\lambda_f} \tag{7}$$

Reliability and availability and among the key factors that are used to define the quality of software in practice. In what follows, we formulate mathematical representations for both these factors.

5.2. Availability

The availability of software can be expressed using cycles of uninterrupted working intervals (Uptime), followed by a repair period after a failure has occurred (Downtime) using (8).

$$A = \frac{Uptime}{Uptime + Downtime} = 1 - \frac{Downtime}{Uptime + Downtime} \tag{8}$$

Considering that availability is typically evaluated over a 1 year period, $Uptime + Downtime = 1\ year = (60 \times 24 \times 365)$ minutes. Therefore, as an example, to achieve system availability of 5 9's (i.e. A = 99.999%) the maximum allowed downtime would be 5.26 minutes/year.

5.3. Reliability

On the other hand, software *reliability* is the probability that the software has not failed after a time period t. Therefore, reliability is a function of t, and can be denoted as R(t). R(t) is typically modeled using an exponential distribution in which the parameter is failure rate λ as shown in Eq. (9)

$$R(t) = 1 - \exp(-\lambda t) \tag{9}$$

It is important to note that while both reliability and availability are a measure of software quality, they have different technical meanings. In particular, availability is determined by both uptime and downtime, while reliability is only influenced by uptime. This implies that two software releases or systems having the same failure rate, would have the same reliability, but might have different availabilities. Achieving a high availability generally requires having automated ways of recovering from failures, for example, through redundancy or rebooting, so that the downtime is minimized. Software failures for which the system is able to automatically recover are known as covered failures. On the other hand, if a system fails to automatically detect and/or recover from a failure, such a failure is known as an uncovered failure, and usually leads to customer perceived defects. In systems where recovery time is significant, a coverage factor – the proportion of all failures that are covered failures – is defined. However, in most practical applications, it requires specialized tools to determine covered failures. Therefore, typical failure counts usually only consider the uncovered defects.

5.4. Discussion

In what follows, we use (anonymised/scaled) data from project A to demonstrate the various aspects of software failure, reliability and availability, together with the predictions that are carried for the same. The data compares multiple releases of a software product over multiple years. Outage data represents unplanned, customer-reported, and uncovered failures, including full and partial outages. The outages were collected across a deployment of over 400 systems. The monthly outage count is annualized and normalized by the number of deployed systems as outages/year/system, which is equivalent to the failure rate. In the same way, the monthly outage downtime is annualized and normalized by deployed systems as downtime/year/deployed system. It should be noted that the downtime duration of each outage is discounted by percentage impact (i.e. 100% being a full outage), using the TL 9000 counting rule.

In **Figure 15**, we show the predicted software reliability as a function of failure rate (on the left) and software availability as a function of annual downtime (on the right). The following observations can be made:

- From one release to another, the actual data generally lies within the 90% confidence limits for both availability and reliability. This is testament to the accuracy of the generated predictions.
- Over time, from one release to the next, we can observe a continuous improvement in software availability and reliability. This is not surprising since it takes time and increased effort to enhance software design, development and test practices.
- There is a slight deterioration in reliability and availability at R5, corresponding to a change in hardware, but these quickly improve again after that. This can be explained by the need to re-design the software, but also demonstrates the important effect hardware can have on the quality of software, i.e. sometimes significant long term improvements in software quality may only be achieved through changes in hardware.
- It is worth observing that predicting availability is generally more difficult than predicting reliability. This is due to the fact that availability is affected by the downtime while reliability is not. In addition, as software development teams get used to a product from one release to the next, they get used to the system, and therefore, are normally able to significantly reduce the average system downtime.

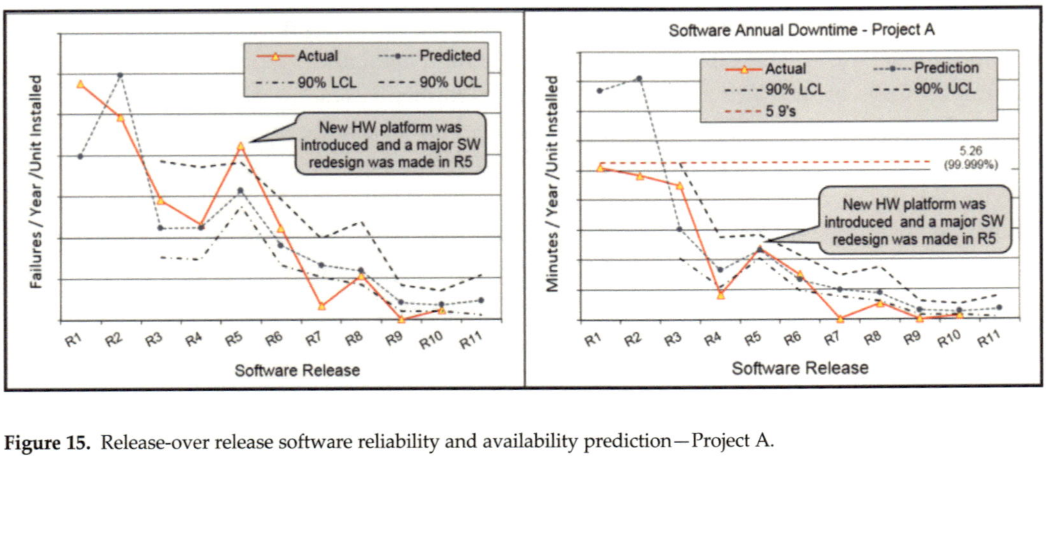

Figure 15. Release-over release software reliability and availability prediction—Project A.

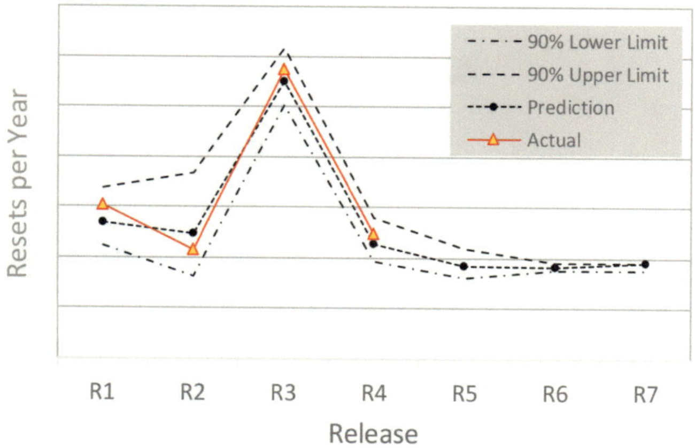

Figure 16. Software failure rate prediction—Project B.

Finally, we applied the method to Project B. In this project, it is not practical to collect the system downtime in the field due to the nature of the product. However, customers are concerned about resets. Therefore, the focus is on the number of unplanned autonomous resets. **Figure 16** summarizes the annual reset rate with prediction and actual data over several releases. The predicted values are remarkably close to actual data and within the 90% limits. Although actual downtime is not available, we can use reset time measured in the lab to calculate the reset-based availability using the reset rate prediction.

6. Implementation

Figure 17 shows the implementation of BRACE. The tool is made up of multiple application programming interfaces (APIs), each of them connecting to a defect logging database (such as JIRA). Defect data is collected from the defect databases in real-time and pre-processed by a computer program (in Python) before being stored into a cloud-based, shared database used by the system. The SRGM algorithm (which is written in Python) then performs the core processing, providing a consistent, fast, flexible, robust, and statistically sound result. Using the output of from core processing, we have also created a unified graphical user interface (GUI) onto which a wealth of software quality metrics are presented to users. While in the current implementation all components of the tool are hosted in a virtual machine running in openstack, it is possible to have them also running in a dedicated server if needed.

As an example use case, for a given project, a number of input parameters are required for the tool. Such inputs include the project milestones, the require changes in defect rate before and after deployment, and a number of assumptions based on expert knowledge of both the product and development process.

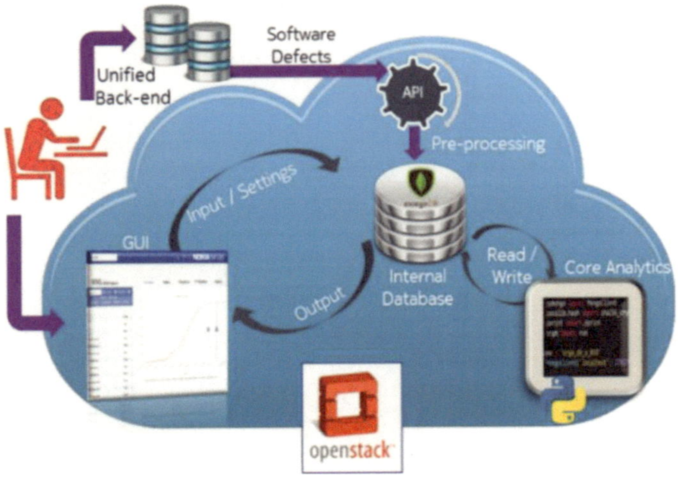

Figure 17. Design and implementation of a cloud-based BRACE.

7. Conclusion

In this chapter we presented a practical approach to software defect prediction, which helps assure the delivery of high quality software. An innovative cloud-based analytics tool, BRACE, was introduced which automates the entire process of data extraction, pre-processing, core processing, and post-processing, combined with a user interface. It no longer relies on the use of a spreadsheet and generates prediction in real-time, which can be shared with any members of a project. SRGM is the core analytics engine which implements technical breakthroughs in this area. It provides a robust, consistent, flexible, fast, statistically sound approach to defect prediction for any defect data sets without human intervention. The enhanced version of SRGM incorporates feature arrival data to provide defect prediction throughout the lifecycle of each release with much improved accuracy. We also demonstrated the method for predicting customer defects and software availability during the operation phase, which should be the basis for software quality assurance. We demonstrated the effectiveness of the approach using data sets taken from telecom development projects, varying from traditional development to DevOps CI/CD with full agile development. This approach can be easily applied to any software development projects.

Author details

Kazu Okumoto[1]*, Rashid Mijumbi[1] and Abhaya Asthana[2]

*Address all correspondence to: kazu.okumoto@nokia-bell-labs.com

1 Nokia Bell Labs, Dublin, Ireland

2 Nokia Bell Labs, Westford, USA

References

[1] Mijumbi R, Serrat J, Gorricho JL, Bouten N, De Turck F, Boutaba R. Network function virtualization: State-of-the-art and research challenges. IEEE Communications Surveys & Tutorials. 2016;**18**(1):236-262

[2] Ozakinci R, Tarhan A. The role of process in early software defect prediction: Methods. In: Attributes and Metrics. Cham: Springer International Publishing; 2016. pp. 287-300. DOI: 10.1007/978-3-319-38980-6 21

[3] Martin LS. Probabilistic models for software reliability prediction. In: Freiberger W, editor. Statistical Computer Performance Evaluation. Academic Press; 1972. pp. 485-502, ISBN 9780122669507, https://doi.org/10.1016/B978-0-12-266950-7.50029-3. (http://www.sciencedirect.com/science/article/pii/B9780122669507500293)

[4] Jelinski Z, Moranda PB. Software reliability research. In: Feiberger W, editor. Statistical Computer Performance Evaluation. New York: Academic; 1972. pp. 465-484

[5] Schick GJ, Wolverton RW. Assessment of software reliability. In: Proceedings of Operations Research. Wurzburg-Wien. 1973. pp.395-422

[6] Schneidewind NF. Analysis of error processes in computer software. In: Proceedings of the International Conference on Reliable Software. IEEE Computer Society; 1975. pp. 337-346

[7] Musa JD. A theory of software engineering and its application. IEEE Transactions on Software Engineering, SE-1. 1975;**3**:312-327

[8] Goel AL, Okumoto K. Time-dependent error-detection rate model for software reliability and other performance measures. IEEE Transactions on Reliability. 1979:206-211

[9] Yamada S, Ohba M, Osaki S. S-shaped reliability growth modeling for software error detection. IEEE Transactions on Reliability. 1983:475-478

[10] Musa JD, Iannino A, Okumoto K. Software Reliability: Measurement, Prediction, Application. New York: McGraw-Hill; 1987

[11] Musa JD. Operational profiles in software-reliability engineering. IEEE Software. 1993: 14-32

[12] Wallace D, Coleman C. Application and improvement of software reliability models. In: Hardware and Software Reliability (323–08). Software Assurance Technology Center (SATC); 2001

[13] Okamura H, Dohi T, Osaki S. A reliability assessment method for software products in operational phase—Proposal of an accelerated life testing model. Electronics and Communications in Japan. 2001:25-33

[14] Jeske DR, Zhang X, Pham H. Adjusting software failure rates that are estimated from test data. IEEE Transactions on Reliability. 2005:107-114

[15] Zhang X, Pham H. Software field failure rate prediction before software deployment. Journal of Systems and Software. 2006:291-300

[16] Okumoto K. Experience report: Practical software availability prediction in telecommunication industry. In: Proceedings of the 27th IEEE International Symposium on Software Reliability Engineering (ISSRE). 2016. pp. 331-342

[17] Asthana A, Okumoto K. Integrative software design for reliability: Beyond models and defect prediction. Bell Labs Technical Journal. 2012;**17**(3):39-62

[18] Lyu MR. Handbook of Software Reliability Engineering. New York: Computer Society Press, Los Alamitos and McGraw-Hill; 1995

[19] Okamura H, Dohi T. SRATS: Software reliability assessment tool on spreadsheet. In: Proceedings of the 24th International Symposium on Software Reliability Engineering (ISSRE 2013). IEEE CPS; 2013. pp. 100-117

[20] Wikipedia. List of Software Reliability Models. https://en.wikipedia.org/wiki/List_of_software_reliability_models

[21] Okumoto K, Mijumbi R, Asthana A. Brace: Cloud-based software reliability assurance. In: 2017 IEEE International Symposium on Software Reliability Engineering Workshops (ISSREW), vol. 00. Oct. 2017. pp. 57-60. [Online]. DOI: ieeecomputersociety.org/10.1109/ISSREW.2017.48

[22] https://en.wikipedia.org/wiki/Q%E2%80%93Q_plot

[23] Kimura M, Toyota T, Yamada S. Economic analysis of software release problems with warranty cost and relaibility requirement. Reliability Engineering & System Safety. 1999: 49-55

[24] Yang B, Xie M. A study of operational and testing reliability in software reliability analysis. Reliability Engineering & System Safety. 2000:323-329

[25] Ukimoto S, Dohi T. A software cost model with reliability constraint under two operational scenarios. International Journal of Software Engineering and Its Applications. 2013; **7**(1)

[26] TL 9000 Measurements Handbook, Release 4.0, 2007, Quality Excellence for Suppliers of Telecommunications (QuEST) Forum, http://www.tl9000.org/handbooks/documents/ProdCat_Tables_4-0.pdf

Chapter 4

Chaos-Based Spectral Keying Technique for Secure Communication and Covert Data Transmission between Radar Receivers over an Open Network Channel

Oleg Zemlyaniy and Konstantin Lukin

Additional information is available at the end of the chapter

http://dx.doi.org/10.5772/intechopen.79027

Abstract

Application of chaotic signals in modern telecommunication facilities and radars is an actual task that can significantly extend functionality of these systems and improve their performance. In this chapter, we propose a concept of chaos-based technique for secure communication and hidden data transmission over an open network channel which is based on a novel method for spectral keying of chaotic signal generated by nonlinear dynamical system with delayed feedback. In the technique developed, the modulating information sequence controls the parameter of nonlinear element, so that it switches the chaotic modes and changes the spectral structure of the signal, transmitted to the communication channel. A noncoherent reception is used for demodulation the information message from received waveform. We start from theoretical justification of the proposed scheme, and show then the numerical simulations and imitation modeling results, as well as demonstrate experimental validation of suggested technique. Also, the communication system reliability and its covert operation efficiency under impact of AWGN in the environment with high-level interferences have been shown by means of evaluation the system anti-jamming capabilities and unauthorized access immunity.

Keywords: chaos-based secure communications, deterministic chaos, nonlinear dynamical system with delayed feedback, chaos generator, chaos modulation, noncoherent receiver, skew tent-map, chaotic map with varying parameter, spectral keying, spectral modulation, spread-spectrum system, wide-band chaotic waveform

1. Introduction

At present, scientific direction on the usage of nonlinear dynamical systems with chaotic regimes for creation of radar and telecommunication systems, the operation principles of which are based on specific features of chaotic signals [1–6], attract increasing attention among hardware engineers and software developers. There are several basic schemes for building systems with chaotic dynamics for information transmission are known today: systems with a Chaotic Masking [7], Chaos Shift Keying (CSK) [8, 9], Nonlinear Mixing [10], Direct Chaotic Modulation (Inverse Systems) [11, 12], Predictive Poincare Control Modulation [13], chaos in systems with phase-locked loop [14] and frequency modulation with a chaotic signal [15]. Systems with a coherent and noncoherent reception are distinguished by the method of extracting the transmitted message from the received signal.

Operation of systems with implementation of coherent method of reception is based on the phenomenon of chaotic synchronization [7–9, 16], that is used for demodulation of chaotic oscillations. As a rule, in systems of this type, in order to achieve synchronous mode, it is necessary to ensure a high degree of identity between the parameters of a transmitter and a receiver. The structure and parameters of the transmitter, in general case, are not known to the third party, which ensures the confidentiality of the transmitted information. The disadvantages of systems with chaotic synchronization relates to the need keeping the identity of the transmitter and receiver parameters, as well as restrictions associated with increased requirements for the quality of communication channel, and low resistance to additive noise.

Examples of systems that do not use the phenomenon of chaotic synchronization include systems that perform Differential Chaos Shift Keying (DCSK) [17, 18], energy reception [19], and an inverse system without chaotic synchronization. In DCSK and systems with an estimation of energy parameters for extracting information from the received signal, its statistical properties are used and traditional methods of signal processing are applied. In this case, high noise immunity is inherent when performing the optimal signal reception.

Among systems with chaos, the delayed feedback systems [20–23] are of particular interest from the point of view of their use for transmission of confidential information (secure communication) [24, 25], in view of the fact that due to their infinite dimensionality they allow generating chaotic signals whose parameters cannot be restored by third party without using special techniques. In addition, because of their broadband, they have potential of greater secure messaging capabilities than low-dimensional chaotic systems [26].

A system of secure information transmission based on a delayed feedback generator operating by means of switching the delay time in the transmitter and extracting an information signal using two different delay systems in the receiver, and each of them is to be synchronized with the received signal (coherent reception), which is proposed in [25]. For communication systems of this type, in which chaotic modes are switched, the presence of noise prevents the full chaotic synchronization between the receiver and the transmitter. Therefore, to increase noise immunity, the authors propose to perform additional processing that reduces the additive noise level in the output signal of the receiver.

http://dx.doi.org/10.5772/intechopen.79027

A broadband channel for digital information transmission based on spectral code modulation, first proposed in [27], is considered in [28], at which the transmitter adds the reference broadband noise signal with its copy delayed for the different time intervals, duration of which depends on incoming information binary symbol. In the receiver, an unambiguous reconstruction of the binary symbol stream occurs when performing double spectral processing of the received signal when estimating the position of the information peak of its autocorrelation function takes place.

In this chapter, we suggest a broadband communication system based on a nonlinear dynamical system with time delay and switching of chaotic regimes in which the information sequence controls the parameter of a nonlinear element by means of keying mode. From our investigations, we found that a result of such controlling procedure is redistribution of the transmitted signal spectral components, which leads to periodic (in frequency) nonuniformity in the signal spectrum. We show that in this case, the position of the maxima and minima on the frequency axis is uniquely determined by the value of the control parameter, that is, the transmitted symbol.

The technique developed is not supposed using chaotic synchronization since communication systems based on the phenomenon of chaotic synchronization have serious drawbacks that limit their real world application. Namely, the main disadvantage of such systems is an extremely bad quality of information signal restoring in the receiver when the parameters of the transmitter and receiver are detuned and when noise and distortions of the signal in the communication channel increase.

In the noncoherent receiver, matched filtration is used to demodulate the transmitted message, which satisfies the optimality criterion for receiving continuous noise waveforms. Data recovery is performed by estimating the envelope amplitudes at the outputs of two parallel comb filters, the amplitude-frequency characteristics of which are matched with the amplitude spectrum of the input signal, and making a decision when comparing them. Thus, the proposed method combines the use of specific features of time-delayed chaotic systems that allow the formation of a chaotic waveform with a periodic structure in the spectral domain and a matched filtration of a wideband chaotic waveform that allows achieving a high signal-to-noise ratio, which ensures good noise immunity of the communication system as a whole.

2. Spectral properties of chaos generated by the delayed feedback system with one-dimensional skew tent map

A nonlinear dynamical system with delayed feedback of the ring type is used for broadband chaotic signal generation. In the general case, under the assumption that the whole system is inertial-free, it is described by a difference equation of the form:

$$x(t) = F[x(t - T_0), r, a], \tag{1}$$

where $F(x,\ r,\ a)$ is the mapping function of the unit interval $[0, 1]$ of the x-axis into itself $F : [0, 1] \mapsto [0, 1]$; r and a are the map parameters defined by the function F; T_0 is the delay time.

The solutions of Eq. (1) and their correlation properties for the case when the function $F(x, r, a)$ defines a unimodal piecewise-linear map (skew tent map):

$$F(x, r, a) = \begin{cases} rx/a, & x \in [0, a] \\ r(1-x)/(1-a), & x \in (a, 1] \end{cases} \tag{2}$$

are investigated by authors in [29].

The evolution of any dynamical system depends on its parameters. Their change leads to an inevitable change in the trajectories of motions of the dynamical system in time. In this case, a small change in the parameters can lead to both an insignificant change in behavior and a significant rearrangement of the phase trajectories (bifurcations). To exploit the map under consideration as source of chaotic sequences, one needs to make selection of its parameters. It is convenient to use a two-parameter bifurcation diagram in terms of the parameters r and a (**Figure 1**).

In **Figure 1**, for the sake of clarity, the step along the parameter a is chosen to be sufficiently large, which, however, does not prevent from following the evolution of the iterative process when a changes. More detailed information is contained in the cross sections of the three-dimensional picture made for fixed values of the parameter r (**Figure 2**).

A characteristic feature that is visible on these cross-sections is the presence of three boundary values of the bifurcation parameter a, under which the picture of the behavior of the system abruptly changes. Therefore, for example, for $r = 0.7$ (**Figure 2(a)**), the fixed point for $a = a_1 = 0.3$ loses stability, that leads to the appearance of cycles of intervals, which merged, when $a = a_1 = 0.5$. With further increase of the bifurcation parameter, the amplitude of the

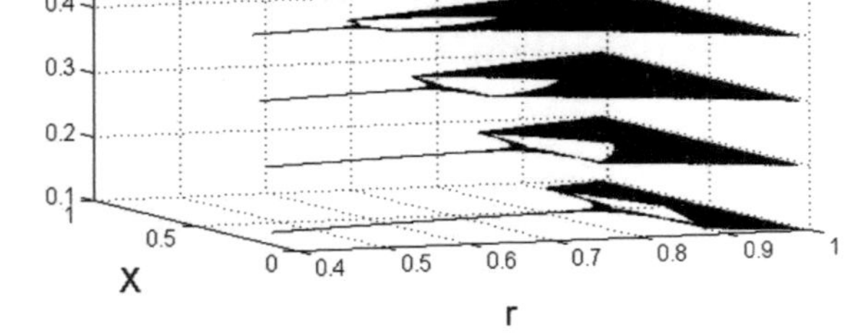

Figure 1. Two-parameter bifurcation diagram of the skew tent map.

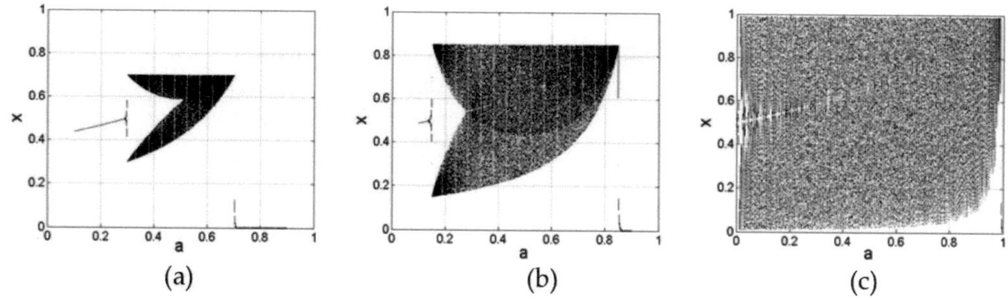

Figure 2. Cross-sections of the two-parameter bifurcation diagram of the skew tent map obtained for parameter r fixed values: (a) $r = 0.7$; (b) $r = 0.9$; (c) $r = 1$.

chaotic oscillations decreases, and when $a = a_1 = 0.7$, a fixed stable point appears and the oscillations disappear.

Since two points of the mapping function graph are fixed, the layout of the graph is completely determined by the position of the top. There are three regions with qualitatively different system states (**Figure 3**) for it.

When the top of the map is in region I (**Figure 3(a)**), the map has two fixed points, one of which is unstable (z_0), and the other is stable (z_1). Therefore, the iterative process converges to z_1. When the top of the map moves to region II (**Figure 3(b)**), the fixed point z_1 loses its stability, since the absolute value of the derivative at this point becomes greater than 1. The z_0 point is still unstable. In this case, a region of chaotic oscillations with dense filling appears on the bifurcation diagram. With the further movement of the top of the map in the direction toward the region III, there comes a moment when the top and the fixed point merge (this occurs on the bisector of the first quadrant) and when the top of the map falls into the region III (**Figure 3(c)**), the oscillations in the system disappear, since there remains one fixed point z_0 that gets stable. Thus, in order to obtain chaotic regimes when choosing bifurcation parameter values r and a, it is necessary to be guided by the condition that the top of the map belongs to the region II.

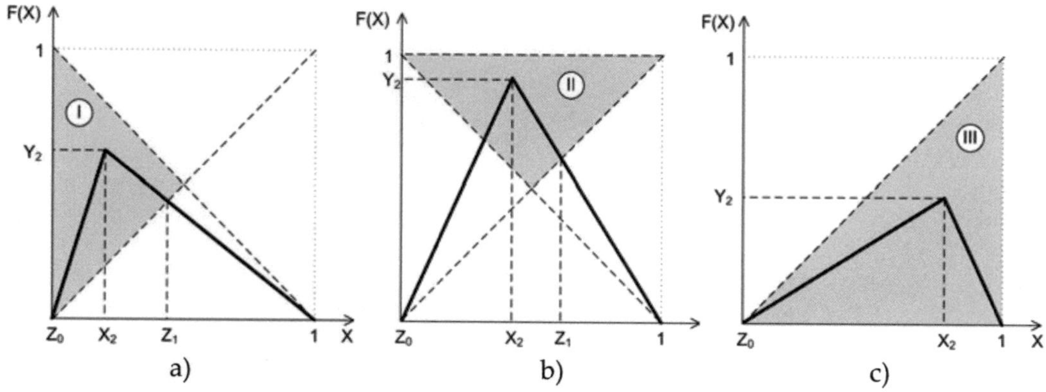

Figure 3. Areas with qualitatively different states of the system.

When choosing oscillation modes in systems with time delay, it is necessary to take into account the stability of oscillations and the influence of external noise [30]. Apparently, under the influence of destabilizing factors, which can be described by the presence of additive or multiplicative noise, the boundary of the chosen region of the bifurcation parameters will be blurred.

Thus, when $r = 1$ (only this case will be considered below), the sequence of iterations of a skew tent map is completely chaotic. Its interesting property is the independence of the invariant measure on the parameter a. As shown in [31, 32], this map is ergodic on the interval $[0, 1]$ and has an invariant measure $p(x) = 1$. This circumstance allows determining exactly the dependence of the Lyapunov exponent on the abscissa of the top of the map. Since the invariant measure is known, averaging over time can be replaced by averaging over x [31] when calculating the characteristic Lyapunov exponent:

$$\sigma = \int p(x) \ln \left| \frac{dF(x)}{dx} \right| dx. \tag{3}$$

Taking into account that in our case, the map is represented by a function that differs from 0 only on the interval $[0, 1]$ and does not take negative values anywhere, after integration, we get $\sigma = -\ln \left[a^a (1-a)^{1-a} \right]$. As seen from the graph of this function (**Figure 4**), the Lyapunov exponent is positive everywhere within unit interval and reaches its maximum value for a symmetric case (for $a = 0.5$). As a criterion for selection the value of parameter a, we choose Lyapunov exponents to be at least 0.5 (white area in **Figure 4**).

It was shown in [29] that the autocorrelation function of the solution of Eq. (1) can be represented in the form

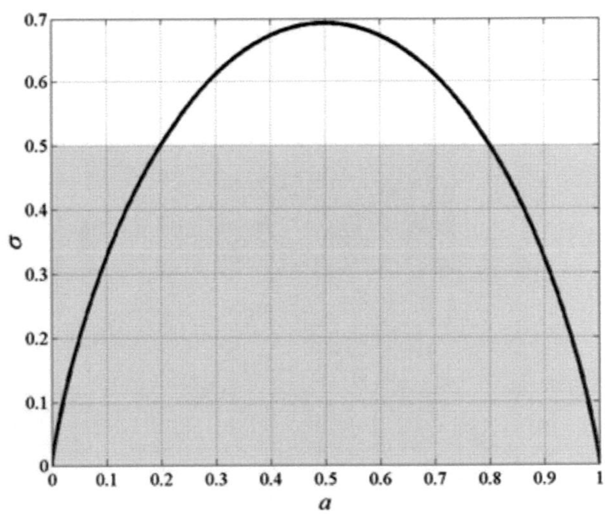

Figure 4. Dependence of the Lyapunov exponent on the asymmetry parameter of a skew tent map.

$$R(\tau) = \int_0^\infty B(t)\delta(\tau - t)\,dt, \tag{4}$$

where $B(t) = \begin{cases} C(t), & t = nT_0, \\ 0, & t \neq nT_0, \end{cases}$ $n \in N$ In this case, the dependence of the autocorrelation function of the solution of Eq. (1) with a nonlinear function Eq. (2) has the following form [33, 34]:

$$C(t) = \begin{cases} C_0 e^{-t/\tau_c}, & a > 1/2 \\ C_0(-1)^t e^{-t/\tau_c}, & a < 1/2 \end{cases}, \tag{5}$$

where $\tau_c = |1/\ln|2a - 1||$. Using the Wiener-Khinchin theorem, we derive the power spectrum of the process with autocorrelation function $R(\tau)$:

$$W(\omega) = 2\int_0^\infty R(\tau)\cos\omega\tau\,d\tau. \tag{6}$$

Substituting Eq. (4) into Eq. (6) and changing the order of integration, we have:

$$W(\omega) = 2\int_0^\infty B(t)\cos\omega t\,dt. \tag{7}$$

Taking into account that the function $B(t)$ differs from zero only at points $t = nT_0$, the integral Eq. (7) can be replaced by the series $W(\omega) = 2\sum_{n=0}^{\infty} C(nT_0)\cos n\omega T_0$, and to calculate the sum of this series we need substitute $C(nT_0)$ by values from Eq. (5). As a result, the problem reduces to calculating the sum of the series $\sum_{k=1}^{\infty}(-1)^k e^{-ky}\cos kx$, where $y > 0$. After carrying out all calculations, we finally obtain that the power spectrum of chaotic process with the autocorrelation function Eq. (4) has the following form (up to a constant factor):

$$W(\omega, a) = \begin{cases} \dfrac{e^{T_0/\tau_c} - \cos\omega T_0}{e^{T_0/\tau_c} + e^{-T_0/\tau_c} - 2\cos\omega T_0}, & 0.5 < a < 1, \\ \dfrac{e^{T_0/\tau_c} + \cos\omega T_0}{e^{T_0/\tau_c} + e^{-T_0/\tau_c} + 2\cos\omega T_0}, & 0 < a < 0.5 \end{cases}. \tag{8}$$

Thus, the power spectrum of chaotic auto-oscillations in the dynamical system of ring type with a delay in the deviation of a nonlinear map from a symmetric form is a periodic function of the frequency with a frequency period $f_T = \omega_T/2\pi = 1/T_0$, corresponding to the delay time T_0 of the signal in the delay line (**Figure 5**).

For $0.5 < a < 1$, the first maximum of the power spectrum is located at zero frequency, while when $0 < a < 0.5$ it is shifted to $f_T/2$ (the maxima are located at frequencies

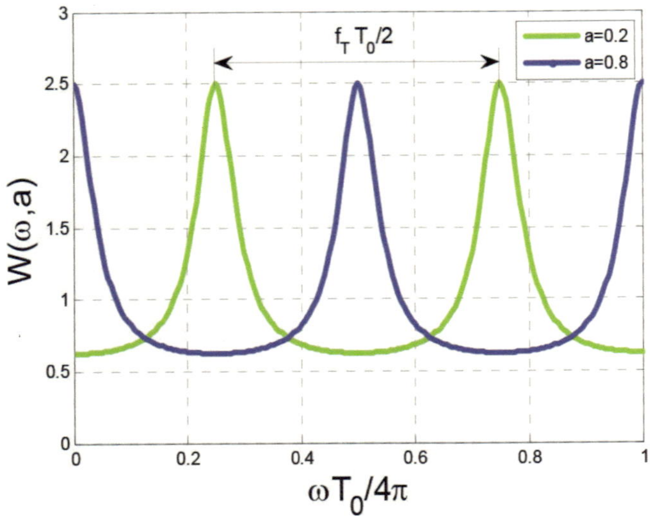

Figure 5. Power spectrum of chaotic oscillations in a ring dynamical system with delay for different values of the parameter *a*.

$1/(2T_0)$,$3/(2T_0)$, ...). Therefore, assigning the control parameter value a from the interval (0, 0.5) or (0.5, 1) allows manipulating the positions of the spectrum maxima, thereby entering information message into a chaotic carrier [35]. To transmit a binary sequence, it is sufficient to use two fixed values of a, for example, following the formula $a = 0.5 + \lambda \text{sign}(s_i - 0.5)$, where s_i is the information bit that takes the value "0" or "1". Here parameter $\lambda \in 0, 1$ determines the ratio between maxima and minima (the "depth" of the irregularity) in the formed spectrum. If the signal generated in this way arrives in the receiver at the input of the comb filter, the frequency response shape of which is matched to the signal spectrum, then the response at the filter output will be maximal in comparison with the case, when the signal with a spectrum that does not match to the filter frequency response acts at the filter input. An analysis of the magnitude of the response allows making decision whether "0" or "1" was transmitted and thus restoring the original information.

3. Simulation modeling of the data transmission system

The efficiency of the proposed method of information transmission was tested by means of simulation using the Simulink environment of the MATLAB software package. We used Eq. (1), written in discrete time domain at $r = 1$ as a source of chaos, controlled by a discrete information sequence:

$$x_n = F(x_{n-M}, a). \tag{9}$$

where $x_1, x_2, \ldots x_M$ is the vector of initial values by dimension M. If a discrete sequence x_n is associated with the binary sequence $s_n = \text{sign}(a - x_n)$, then discrete Eq. (9) with the nonlinear function Eq. (2) has the following form:

$$x_n = \frac{2x_{n-M} + s_{n-M} - 1}{2a + s_{n-M} - 1}. \quad (10)$$

Following this formula, the problem of generating a chaotic signal in discrete time domain using a dynamical system with delayed feedback and a nonlinear function Eq. (2) reduces to computing the samples of the sequence exploiting the algorithm given by formula Eq. (10). Entering information into a chaotic signal is accomplished by changing the parameter a value. In this case, the computational algorithm consists of a block of delay for M samples and a set of functional blocks performing elementary arithmetic operations. This allows implementation of a digital synthesis module based on FPGA technology, for example, using standard elements of the "Xilinx System Generator for DSP" and "ISE Foundation" libraries [36]. The simulation model of proposed chaos communication system is presented in **Figure 6**.

Signal is generated in the transmitter as follows. We choose a binary sequence whose elements s_i take the values "0" or "1" as a test information signal $S(t)$. The information signal controls the switching element, which changes the parameter of the nonlinear function (**Figure 7**), herewith the parameter values $a_0 = 0.25$ and $a_1 = 0.75$ correspond to transmission of the symbols "0" and "1", respectively.

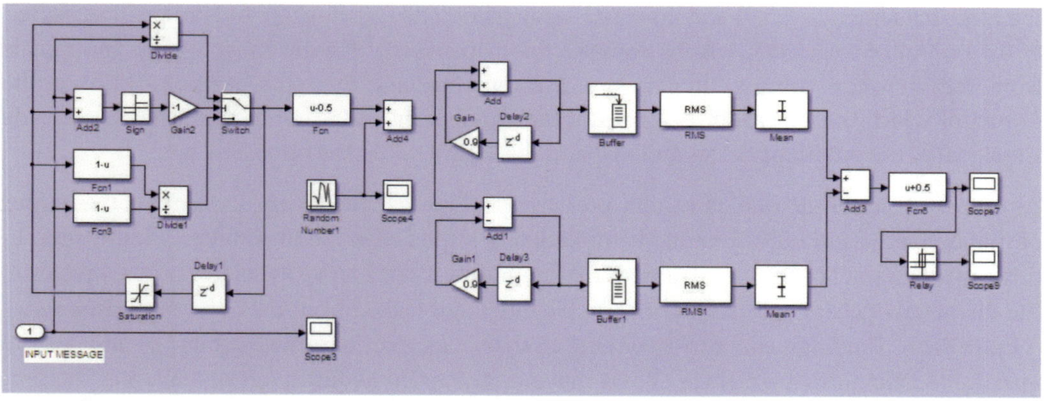

Figure 6. Simulation model of proposed chaos-based communication system.

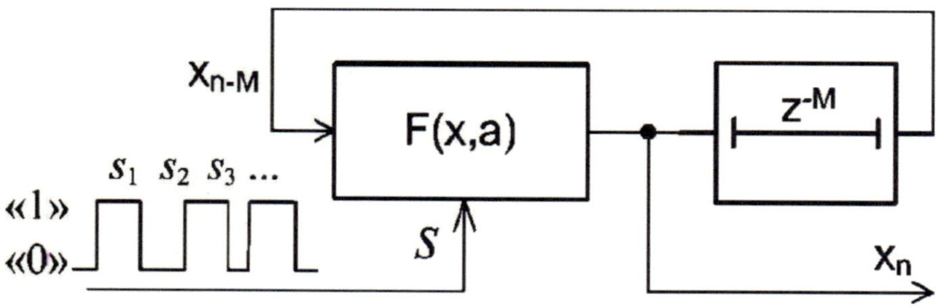

Figure 7. The dynamical system of ring type with a variable parameter of a nonlinear element as a driver of a chaotic signal in the transmitter.

To transmit one information symbol of duration T_S, it is necessary to fulfill the condition $T_S > T_0 >> \Delta t$, where T_0 is the delay time equal to the analysis time of the signal spectrum at the receiver, Δt is the duration of one sample of the chaotic carrier (one information symbol is transmitted for a sequence of $M = T_S/\Delta t$ samples of the chaotic signal). During transmission of the symbol "0" a continuous chaotic signal enters the communication channel, in the spectrum of which the positions of maxima are determined from the condition $\Omega_n^0 = (2n - 1) \pi/T_0$, $n \in N$. When symbol "1" is transmitted, the maxima in the spectrum of the transmitted signal correspond to the condition $\Omega_n^1 = 2(n - 1)\pi/T_0$, $n \in N$.

In the receiver, to derive the information from a chaotic signal, its analysis in the spectral domain is used. A signal with a structural feature of the spectrum in the form of equidistantly located spectral density maxima can be efficiently distinguished with a comb filter, the transmission coefficient modulus of which is $|K(\omega)| = 1/\sqrt{1 + G^2 - 2G\cos\omega T_0}$, where G and T_0 are the amplifier gain and the delay time in the feedback loop, respectively. For a positive value G, the filter frequency response is matched to the chaotic signal spectrum at $0.5 < a < 1$ (transmission of information bit "1"), whereas for its negative value the filter frequency response is matched to the chaotic signal spectrum at $0 < a < 0.5$ (transmission of information bit "0").

The received signal is simultaneously feed two comb filters, one of which has a positive gain in the feedback loop ($G_1 = 0.9$) and the other has negative one ($G_2 = -0.9$). A detector is connected at the output of each filter, which estimates the dispersion of the incoming signal. The signals from both detectors come to the inputs of a comparator and then to a decision device, at the output of which the logical "0" is formed if the signal at the output of the first channel exceeds the signal at the output of the second one and the logical "1" in the opposite case.

As follows from the simulation results, presented in **Figure 8**, the binary sequence at the output of the receiver (**Figure 8(f)**) repeats the modulating sequence in the transmitter (**Figure 8(a)**). In this case, the signal of the transmitter in the communication channel looks like noise waveform, the moments of changing the information bits are not detected from the observable time series (**Figure 8(b)**). The fragments corresponding to transmission of information bits "0" and "1" are visually indistinguishable, which allows making conclusion about covert operation of the proposed method of information transmission.

To study noise immunity, an AGWN channel was modeled by adding a Gaussian white noise to the transmitted waveform. **Figure 8(d)** and **(e)** show the output signal coming from the comparator output for the case when the signal at the receiver input is completely hidden by noise (signal-to-noise ratio is $S/N = -6\ dB$ and $-12\ dB$, correspondingly). Simulation results show that with the system parameters selected, that provide the time-bandwidth product $B \approx 500$, information recovery occurs correctly at the signal-to-noise ratios of at least $-14\ dB$. With a further increase in the power of additive interference, the envelopes at the output in each channel have an unacceptably large dispersion, resulting in false triggering of the key circuit in the decoder at the receiver output leading errors in the information bit sequence recovering.

The use of a delayed feedback system as a source of chaotic carrier allows simplifying the scheme of a transmitter with switching chaotic modes compared to, for example, the device

http://dx.doi.org/10.5772/intechopen.79027

described in [26], where the procedure for forming a spectrum with alternating maxima and minima applies to a pre-generated noise signal. In our approach, a special feature of the spectral characteristics of oscillations in a system with delayed feedback of ring type was used for this, which eliminated the need to include additional signal conversion units to obtain the spectrum of the required shape.

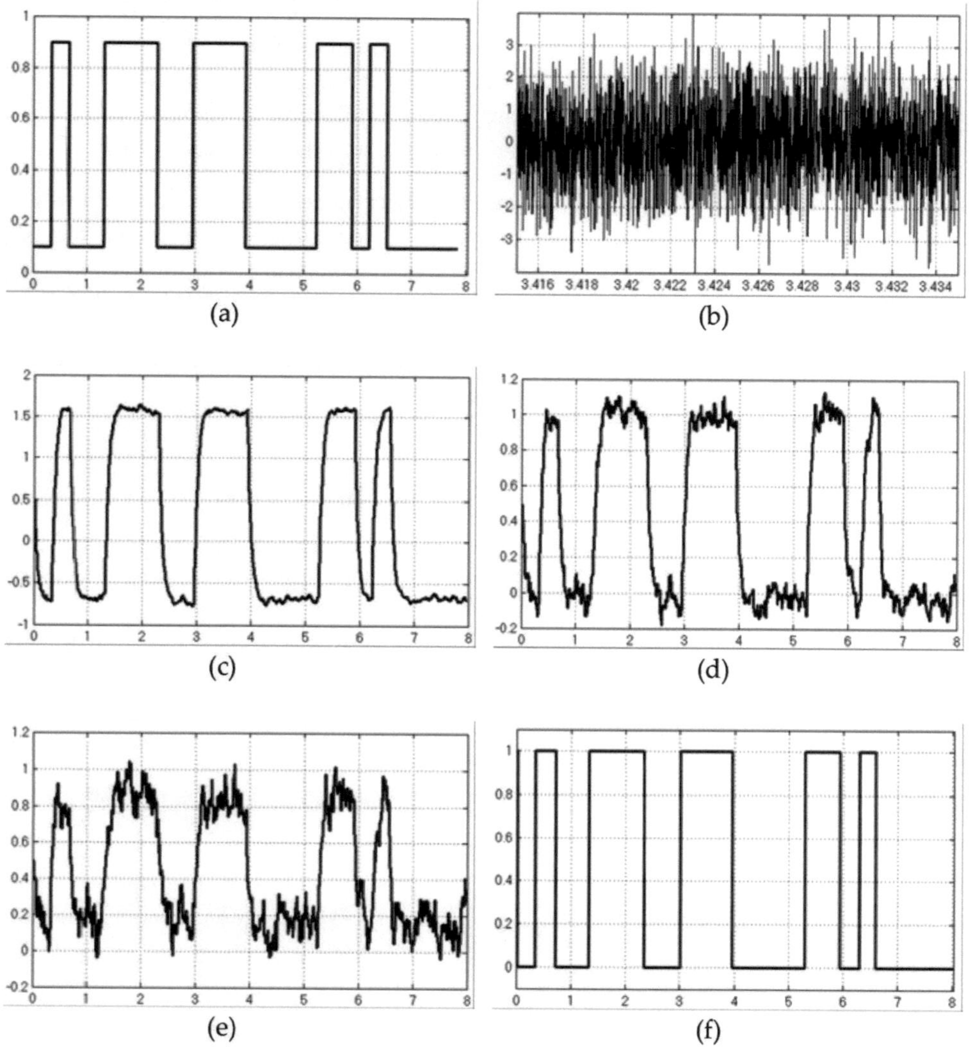

Figure 8. Results of simulation modeling: (a) initial information impulse sequence corresponding to the transmitted message; (b) a fragment of the time series of the signal in the communication channel during the sequential transmission of "1" and "0"; (c) signal at the output in the absence of interference in the communication channel; (d) output signal under the influence of additive Gaussian white noise in the communication channel with a level of +6 dBrelative to the signal level; (e) output signal under the influence of additive Gaussian white noise in the communication channel with a level of +12 dB relative to the signal level; (f) restored information sequence.

4. Experiment on information transmission by the method of spectral keying

The scheme of the experiment on the transmission of a binary message based on the spectral keying of a broadband chaotic signal is shown in **Figure 9**. Designations on the picture as is following: $F(x, s)$ is a block of a nonlinear function, Z^{-M} is a delay unit for M samples, AWG is an arbitrary waveform generator, ADC is an analog-to-digital converter, G1 and G2 are multipliers by a constant, D1 and D2 are blocks of variance estimation, C is a comparator. Functionally, it consists of a software module for calculating samples of a chaotic signal containing the information being transmitted, an AWG board, a communication channel, an ADC board, a software module for extracting the transmitted message from the received signal.

In the AWG module, the preloaded signal samples are extracted from the memory cells with the clock frequency of 4 GHz and feed the DAC input, at the output of which an analog signal is transmitted to the communication channel, which is a coaxial cable with a wave impedance of 50 Ω. An arbitrary waveform generator from Euvis company (California, USA), model AWG472 [37] (**Figure 10**) was used in experimental set-up.

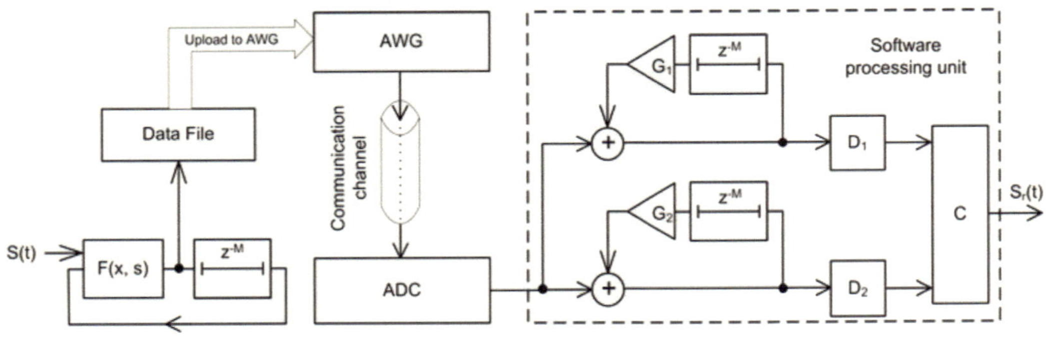

Figure 9. Experimental set-up of communication system for data transmission based on the spectral manipulation of a broadband chaotic signal.

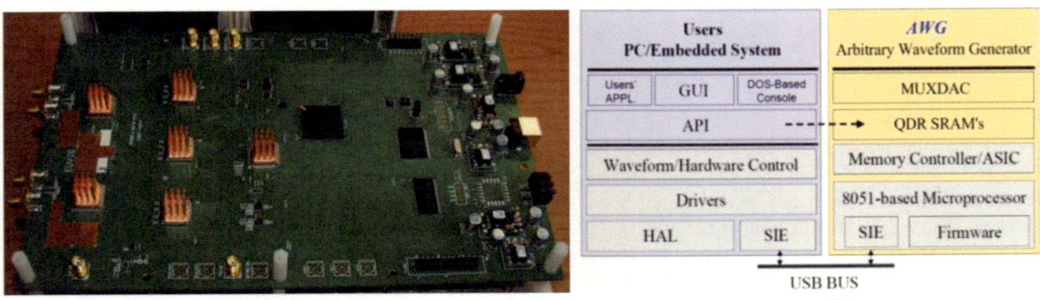

(a) (b)

Figure 10. AWG472 board general appearance (a), AWG472 architecture (b).

The signal received from the communication channel feed the input of the ADC board. Further, digital representation of the received signal is recorded in the memory of a personal computer and processed according to an algorithm that includes the following software modules: two digital recursive filters of the first order operating in parallel; blocks of variance estimation; the comparator [38]. The algorithm for restoring the information sequence is as follows. During the information bit "0" a filter, in which the gain in the feedback circuit has a negative value, is matched with the signal spectrum. During the information bit "1" a filter with a positive coefficient in the feedback circuit is matched with the signal spectrum. By comparing signal variances at the filters outputs within a time interval T_0 corresponding to the number of samples M, an information sequence is extracted from the chaotic signal.

Manchester coding of information bits produce sequence of rectangular pulses. It is used as a test information signal, representing binary word "11,001,110" for experimental evaluation of the system performance. Initial and reconstructed information sequences are shown in **Figure 11**.

As can be seen from the figure, the restored sequence of pulses at the output of the receiver module (red dashed line in **Figure 11(b)**) is identical to the initial information sequence arriving at the information input of the transmitter (**Figure 11(a)**); time lag between these two sequences has fixed value, which is determined by the length of the communication channel, as well as internal delays in the transmitter and receiver modules.

It should be noted that this method used for information transmission does not require chaotic synchronization. The necessary condition for high fidelity of transmitted message recovery is the exact coincidence of the delay time in the transmitter and the delay time in feedback circuit of each of the comb filters used to reconstruct the information sequence at the receiver.

There is a speed limitation in the proposed method for data transmission due to the existence of the minimum allowable time interval necessary for the receiver to correctly recognize the transmitted symbol after the transient processes that occurs due to change of one chaotic regime to another. This is inherent feature for all chaotic systems with mode switching. The accumulation time, necessary for the receiver to estimate the variance of the envelope of the elementary

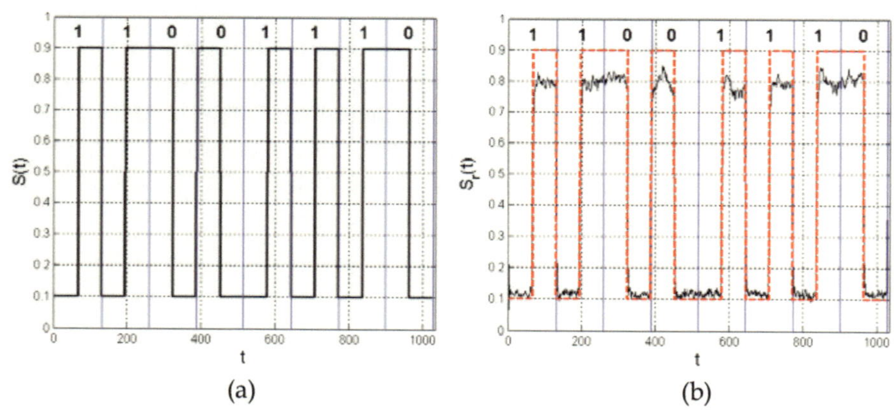

Figure 11. Initial (a) and reconstructed (b) information sequences.

fragments of the signal from which the information sequence is formed, is finite for the duration of one transmitted symbol. It determines the minimum duration of one information bit.

The algorithm of the system operation can be constructed in such a way that at certain time intervals, the predetermined control code sequences will be analyzed by the receiver. If they are misidentified due to distortion during propagation through the channel, a decision will be made to slow down the transmission rate, which will allow the detectors to accumulate for a longer period of time. If necessary, it can be possible to periodically link the operation of the clock generators of the transmitter and the receiver to achieve their matched work by transferring the control code sequences.

5. Conclusions

In this chapter, we have presented theoretical justification, simulation model and experimental results for the physical layer for secure data transmission aiming application in telecommunications and radar sensor networks. We have elaborated technique for information transmission using a wideband chaotic signal generated by a nonlinear time-delayed dynamical system. A novel method, proposed by authors for the first time, differs from the previously known ones in that a feature of chaotic systems is used, consisting in the possibility of forming a periodic structure in the signal spectrum directly during the process of its generation. In the transmitter, constructed according to the chaotic mode switching scheme, the information sequence controls the parameter of the nonlinear element, as a result of which the spectrum structure of the signal transmitted to the communication channel changes. In a noncoherent receiver, which does not require chaotic synchronization with the transmitter, an algorithm for decoding an information message is implemented which is close to optimal, that allows achieving noise immunity and high fidelity of data recovery. As a result of the simulation, the workability of the proposed technique has been demonstrated. We show that the correct recovery of the transmitted binary message is possible at the level of additive broadband Gaussian interference in the communication channel, which considerably exceeds the level of the useful chaotic signal. The operability of the information transmission system based on the spectral keying of a chaotic signal using the proposed algorithm is demonstrated by authors experimentally that confirmed theoretical and modeling findings. The signal processing in the transmitter and receiver are performed in discrete time domain that makes suggested technique ready for DSP and FPGA implementation. The presented results are supposed to be used in development of secure communication systems and radar sensor networks with protection of transmitted information from unauthorized access.

Acknowledgements

This research is partially sponsored by the NATO Science for Peace and Security Programme under grant G5465 (http://www.nato.int/science).

Author details

Oleg Zemlyaniy* and Konstantin Lukin

*Address all correspondence to: zolvas@ukr.net

Laboratory for Nonlinear Dynamics of Electronic Systems (LNDES), O.Ya. Usikov Institute for Radiophysics and Electronics, National Academy of Sciences of Ukraine, Kharkov, Ukraine

References

[1] Kaddoum G. Wireless chaos-based communication systems: A comprehensive survey. IEEE Access. 2016;**4**:2621-2648. DOI: 10.1109/access.2016.2572730

[2] Lukin KA. Noise radar technology: The principles and short overview. Appl. Radio Electronics. 2005;**4**(1):4-13

[3] Kislov VY, Kislov VV. A novel class of signals for communications systems: Wideband chaotic signals. Journal of Communications Technology and Electronics. 1997;**42**(8):897-906

[4] Lukin KA, Shcherbakov VY, Shcherbakov DV. New method for generation of quasi-orthogonal chaotic sequences. Appl. Radio Electronics. 2013;**12**(1):17-24

[5] Kennedy MP, Rovatti R, Setti G, editors. Chaotic Electronics in Telecommunications. Boca Raton, Florida, USA: CRC Press; 2000. 445 p

[6] Dmitriev AS, Panas AI, Starkov SO. Dynamical chaos as paradigm of modern telecommunications. Achievements of Modern Radioelectronics. 1997;**10**:4-26 (in Russian)

[7] Cuomo K, Oppenheim A. Circuit implementation of synchronized chaos with application to communications. Physical Review Letters. 1993;**71**(1):65-68. DOI: https://doi.org/10.1103/PhysRevLett.71.65

[8] Parlitz U, Chua LO, Kocarev L, Halle KS, Shang A. Transmission of digital signals by chaotic synchronization. International Journal on Bifurcation and Chaos. 1992;**2**(4):973-977. DOI: 10.1142/S0218127492000562

[9] Dedieu H, Kennedy MP, Hasler M. Chaos shift keying modulation and demodulation of a chaotic carrier using Self-synchronizing Chua's circuits. IEEE Transactions on Circuits and Systems. 1993;**40**(10):634-642. DOI: 10.1109/82.246164

[10] Dmitriev AS, Panas AI, Starkov SO. Experiments on speech and music signals transmission using chaos. International Journal on Bifurcation and Chaos. 1995;**5**(4):1249-1254. DOI: 10.1142/S0218127495000910

[11] Feldman U, Hasler M, Schwarz W. Communication by chaotic signals: The inverse system approach. International journal on circuit theory and applications. 1996;**24**(5):551-579. DOI: 10.1002/(SICI)1097-007X(199609/10)24:5<551::AID-CTA936>3.0.CO;2-H

[12] Ryabov VB, Usik PV, Vavriv DM. Chaotic masking without synchronization. Radio Physics and Radio Astronomy. 1997;**2**(4):473-479

[13] Schweizer J, Kennedy MP. Predictive Poincare control: A control theory for chaotic systems. Physical Review E. 1995;**52**(5):4865-4876. DOI: 10.1103/PhysRevE.52.4865

[14] Kolumban G, Vizvari R. Nonlinear dynamics and chaotic behavior of sampling phase-locked loops. IEEE Transactions on Circuits and Systems. 1994;**41**(4):333-337. DOI: 10.1109/81.285692

[15] Volkovskii AR, Young SC, Tsimring LS, Rulkov NF. Multi-user communication using chaotic frequency modulation. In: Proceedings of the International Symposium on Nonlinear Theory and its Applications (NOLTA'01); October 28–November 1, 2001; Miyagi. Japan. pp. 561-564

[16] Pecora LM, Carroll TL. Synchronization in chaotic systems. Physical Review Letters. 1990; **64**(8):821-824. DOI: 10.1103/PhysRevLett.64.821

[17] Kaddoum G, Richardson F, Gagnon F. Design and analysis of a multi-carrier differential chaos shift keying communication system. IEEE Transactions on Communications. 2013; **61**(8):3281-3291. DOI: 10.1109/TCOMM.2016.2538236

[18] Xu WK, Wang L, Kolumban G. A novel differential chaos shift keying modulation scheme. International Journal of Bifurcation and Chaos. 2011;**21**(03):799-814. DOI: 10.1142/S0218127411028829

[19] Dmitriev AS, Efremova EV, Kletsov AV, Kuz'min LV, Laktyushkin AM, Yu V, Yurkin VY. Broadband wireless communications and sensor networks. Journal of Communications Technology and Electronics. 2008;**53**(10):1206-1216 (in Russian). DOI: 10.1134/S1064226908100070

[20] Mogel A, Schwarz W, Lukin KA, Zemlyaniy OV. Chaotic wide band oscillator with delay Line. In: Proceedings of the 3rd International Specialist Workshop on Nonlinear Dynamics (NDES'95), 28–29 July 1995; Dublin, Ireland. pp. 259-262

[21] Lukin KA, Maistrenko YL, Sharkovsky AN, Shestopalov VP. The difference equation method in the resonator with nonlinear reflector. Doklady AN SSSR. 1989;**309**(2):327-331 (in Russian)

[22] Lukin KA. High-frequency oscillations from Chua's circuit. Journal of Circuits, Systems and computers. 1993;**3**(2):627-643. DOI: 10.1142/S0218126693000393

[23] Sharkovsky AN. Chaos from a time-delayed Chua's circuits. IEEE Transactions on Circuits and Systems – I: Fundamental Theory and Applications. 1993;**40**(10):781-783. DOI: 10.1109/81.246152

[24] Kye WH. Information transfer via implicit encoding with delay time modulation in a time-delay system. Physics Letters A. 2012;**376**:2663-2667. DOI: 10.1016/j.physleta.2012.07.015

[25] Ponomarenko VI, Karavaev AS, Glukhovskaya EE, Prokhorov MD. Hidden data transmission based on time-delayed feedback system with switched delay time. Technical Physics Letters. 2012;**38**(1):51-54. DOI: 10.1134/ S1063785012010129

[26] Perez G, Cerdeira HA. Extracting messages masked by chaos. Physical Review Letters. 1995;**74**(11):1970-1973. DOI: 10.1103/PhysRevLett.74.1970

[27] Kalinin VI. Spectral modulation of wide-band noise signals. Journal of Communications Technology and Electronics. 1996;**41**(4):488-493 (in Russian)

[28] Kalinin VI. Ultra-wideband data transmission with double spectral processing of noise waveforms. Technical Physics Letters. 2005;**31**(11):929-931. DOI: 10.1134/1.2136955

[29] Zemlyaniy OV, Lukin KA. Correlation-spectral properties of chaos in the nonlinear dynamical system with delayed feedback and asymmetric nonlinear map. Telecommunications and Radio Engineering. 2003;**60**(7–9):137-149. DOI: 10.1615/TelecomRadEng.v60.i789.180

[30] Mackey MC, Nechaeva IG. Noise and stability in differential delay equations. Journal of Dynamics and Differential Equations. 1994;**6**(3):395-426 (in Russian)

[31] Lichtenberg AJ, Lieberman MA. Regular and Stochastics Motion. New York: Springer-Verlag; 1983. 499 p. DOI: 10.1007/978-1-4757-4257-2

[32] Schuster HG, Just W. Deterministic Chaos: An Introduction. 4th ed. Verlag GmbH & Co. KGaA: Wiley-VCH; 2005. 312 p. DOI: 10.1002/3527604804

[33] Grossmann S, Thomae S. Invariant distribution and stationary correlation functions of one-dimensional discrete processes. Zeitschrift für Naturforschung. 1977;**32a**:1353-1363

[34] Sochnev SV. The construction of one-dimensional maps with given stochastic properties. Izvestiya VUZ. Applied Nonlinear Dynamics. 1993;**1**(1,2):63-71 (in Russian)

[35] Zemlyaniy OV. Keying of the broadband chaotic signal spectrum for data transmission. Telecommunications and Radio Engineering. 2016;**75**(5):401-411. DOI: 10.1615/TelecomRadEng.v75.i5.20

[36] System Generator for DSP [Internet]. Available from: https://www.xilinx.com/products/design-tools/vivado/integration/sysgen.html [Accessed: 2018-04-17]

[37] Arbitrary waveform generator AWG472 [Internet]. Available from: http://www.euvis.com/products/mod/awg/awg472.html [Accessed: 2018-04-17]

[38] Lukin KA, Zemlyaniy OV. Digital generation of wideband chaotic signal with the comb-shaped spectrum for communication systems based on spectral manipulation. Radioelectronics and Communications Systems. 2016;**59**(9):417-422

Chapter 5

Optical Amplifiers for Next-Generation Telecommunication

Toto Saktioto and Roby Ikhsan

Additional information is available at the end of the chapter

http://dx.doi.org/10.5772/intechopen.79941

Abstract

The continuing growth of telecommunication networks is currently dominated by fiber optics (or optical networking). Optical fiber has become the guided medium of choice in telecommunications, and associated optoelectronic technologies have become important such as optical fiber itself and optical amplifiers. Optical amplifiers can operate in the long distance using fiber optic carrying data and information in communication links. Some mechanisms are able to amplify electromagnetic signal corresponding to kinds of optical amplifiers. In doped fiber amplifiers and bulk laser sources, a stimulated emission in the amplifier's gain media causes amplification of incoming electromagnetic spectrum. In semiconductor optical amplifier (SOA), electron-hole interaction will occur. For Raman amplifier (RA), its scattering of incoming source with phonons in the lattice of the gain media will produce photons coherent with the incoming photons. Using the simulation, both amplifiers are simulated and compared by in-line amplifiers to allow and keep a better signal from material and geometry disturbance.

Keywords: fiber optic, SOA, FRA, optical amplifier, BER, Q-factor

1. Introduction

Optical amplifiers are optical active components as a circuit enabling technology for optical communication networks. Together with telecommunication system and technology allowing the transmission of channels over the fiber, optical amplifiers have made it possible to transmit many data over distances from 100 km and up to transoceanic distances, providing the data capacity required for current and future communication networks. Optical amplifiers have important role in optical telecommunication and data information. They can be used as repeater circuit in long-distance optical fiber component and cables carrying the world's telecommunication links.

The main aim of this topic is to provide a description of optical amplifiers having a device that amplifies an optical signal, without the need to convert it to an electrical signal or source. This can be formed in visible or invisible electromagnetic spectral source such as light or a laser without an optical resonator, or one in which feedback from the cavity is suppressed. A fundamental optical communication link comprises a transmitter and receiver, with an optical fiber cable and connector which connect them. Even though signals propagating in fiber suffer far less energy in terms of absorption and other damped along the media, such conductor media still have a limit of about 140 km on the distance the signal wave can propagate before producing the disturbance like noise. Before going to the market, the optical amplifiers are necessary to regenerate the optical signals every 80–140 km [1] electronically in order to fulfill the transmission value over long distances. This process describes the receiving of the information signal, organizing and multiplying the amplification optically and electronically, and then retransmitting it over the next medium and segment of the circuit and link. It can be feasible if a single low optical signal is transmitted; it will travel fast and be unfeasible, transmitting in tens of high-capacity order of wavelength-division multiplexing (WDM) channel devices. This results in high-cost, power-hungry, and bulky regenerator port. Furthermore, the regeneration hardware and software depend upon bit-rate, protocol, channel numbers, and modulation which are set to each channel. Any upgrade to the link therefore will automatically require upgrades to the regenerator stations. On the other hand, an ideal amplifier is modeled and designed to amplify any input optical signal directly, no need to transform the signal first to an electronic one.

There are different kinds of processes that can be applied to amplify electromagnetic signals corresponding to the major formation of amplifier optics. For doped fiber ones and bulk lasers, SOA, electron-hole interaction process and recombination will occur. For RA, its scattering of incoming electromagnetic signal with phonons in the lattice of the gain media will produce photons coherent with the incoming photons. Parameters of amplifiers use parametric amplification. **Figure 1** shows amplifier's gain medium causes amplification of incoming light. In semiconductor optical, the block diagram of an amplified signal was optically totally different from an electronic signal regeneration regime, in which channels are usually split, detected, amplified, cleaned electronically, retransmitted, and then recombined. This is a benefit of optical amplifier that can be used to all channels optically and transparently amplified together.

Optical transmission media greatly affect the performance of a communication system. Fiber optic is one of the transmission media that is capable of transmitting information with a large capacity, is high speed, and has low attenuation. Although optical fiber provides many advantages, there are also disadvantages that can disrupt the performance of the fiber optics,

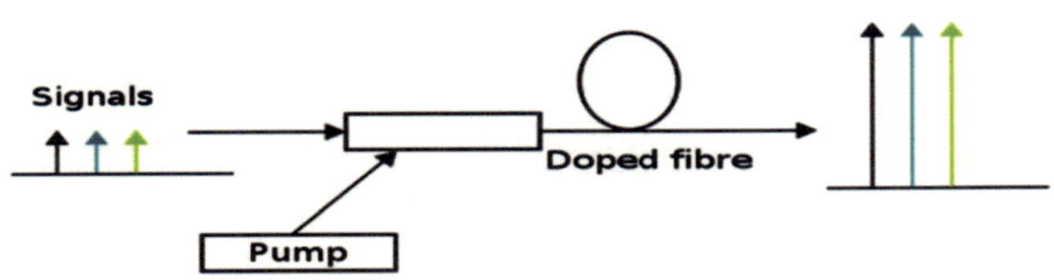

Figure 1. An optical amplifier, all channels are optically, transparently amplified together.

the effects that can limit the delivery and speed of data transmission. This effect is divided into linear effects and nonlinear effects. Linear effects include attenuation and dispersion, a distortion in the beam of light passing through the optical fiber core caused by different modes, wavelengths, and velocities, while nonlinear effects arise due to Kerr effect in the form of self-phase modulation (SPM), cross-phase modulation (XPM), and four-wave mixing (FWM) and as the result of inelastic scattering including stimulated Raman scattering (SRS) and stimulated Brillouin scattering (SBS) [2]. These linear and nonlinear effects can damage information signals such as widespread light pulses, reduced bandwidth shortened, transmission distance, and limited bit-rate. All this is a communication disorder.

2. Optical amplifier properties

Optical amplifiers have several properties. First, it has a gain that the input optical signal is amplified and that is detected from the output port one. It is typically measured in the range of 5–35 dB. For instance if the gain is 10 dB, meaning the input signal is amplified by a factor of 10 subject to logarithm factor. It is also characterized by the supported input and output powers. Especially, the main specification of the amplifier is the maximum output power, which can be contributed and subjected to as saturated output power. There are two kinds of optical amplifiers. They are single and multichannel. The former is designed to amplify only one channel located within a specified band, such as the C-band (1528–1564 nm). This channel can usually deal with over a wide range of gains and require relatively low output power. In the latter channel, WDM amplifiers are designed to work out if any number of channels are input to the amplifier. The gain flatness is the properties of WDM amplifiers, the variation of the gain for different channels, as depicted in **Figure 2** (right side). When the gain is not flat, different WDM channels will have different gains, which can accumulate along a chain of amplifiers leading to a large mismatch between channels. To maintain flat gain, most low-end WDM amplifiers only support a single gain, or a relatively narrow gain range, supporting

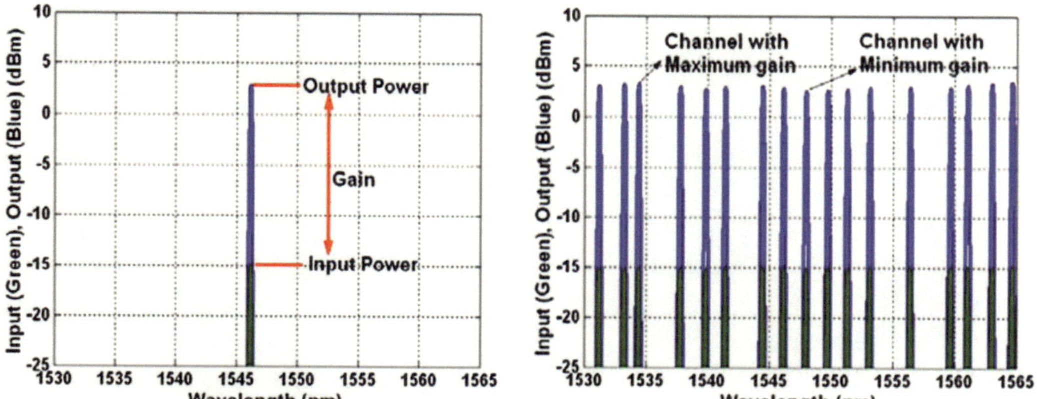

Figure 2. Example input (green) and output (blue) spectrums of a single channel amplifier (left) and a WDM multichannel amplifier (right) [1].

both flat gain and a large gain range, providing a large dynamic input power range, to support different input conditions where any number of channels 1 up to 80 may be available. The maximum quantity of WDM channel amplifiers requires a relatively high saturated output power, particularly in the range of 17–23 dBm. Secondly, optical amplifiers have noise during the amplification process. The noise is detected by its noise figure (NF), where it has the ratio between the signal-to-noise ratio (SNR) at the output port and an ideal SNR at the input port. Due to one-to-one connection between the NF and the optical link, the value of NF should be maintained as low as possible. The value of NF depends upon the technology applied and used for it, where higher gain usually has lower NF. Thirdly, amplifiers detection to dynamical conversion at input port source describe that the gain ideally should not convert at all if the source of input power converts it. But, it is impossible if the amplifier deals with at or almost the peak output power source. This has an important reason if the amplifier can respond step by step; hence its gain is determined only by the average input power source, and it does not influence and change fast (for instance, due to data modulation). Amplifiers having responses too quick can result too noisy. It cannot overcome the multiple channels well.

Optical amplifiers may be used within an optical network as boosters, line amplifiers, or pre-amplifiers, as shown in **Figure 3**, with slightly different specifications.

2.1. Laser amplifier

Generally, laser active gain medium can be pumped to produce gain for spectral wave of a laser made with the same material as its gain medium to result in very high-power laser systems, such as regenerative and chirped-pulse amplifiers which are applied to amplify ultrashort pulses. In addition, solid-state amplifiers are examples of using a wide range of doped solid-state materials (Yb:YAG, Ti:Sa, Nd:YAG) and other kind of sizes and geometries for instance a disk, a slab, and a rod. The variety of materials allows the amplification of different wavelengths, while the shape of the medium can distinguish between what is more suitable for energy [3]. Doped fiber amplifiers (DFAs) use a doped fiber optics having gain resonator to multiply the signals corresponding to the source of fiber lasers. The signals will be multiplied and amplified, and a pump laser is multiplexed to the resonator. The signal will interact through the doping ions (erbium-doped fiber amplifier, EDFA), where the core of a silica fiber is doped with trivalent erbium ions and can be efficiently pumped with a laser at a wavelength of infrared region.

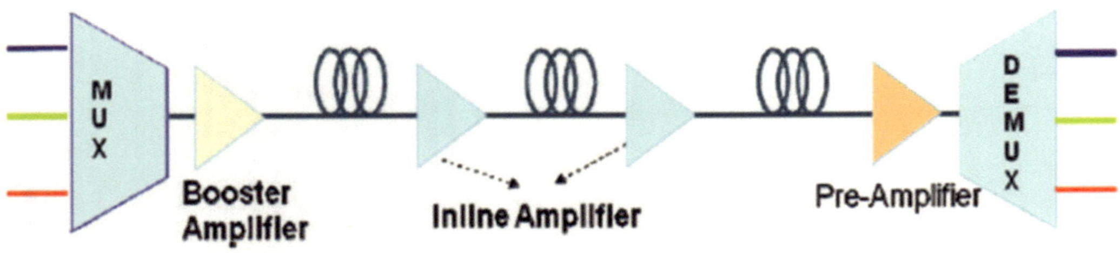

Figure 3. A simple WDM optical network, where a number of transmitted channels are combined using a WDM multiplexer (MUX), amplified using a booster amplifier before being launched into the transmission fiber, re-amplified every 80–120 km using in-line amplifiers, and finally preamplified before being demultiplexed and received [1].

http://dx.doi.org/10.5772/intechopen.79941

Amplification is obtained by processing of emission which is stimulated and producing photons in the dopant ions in the optical fiber which is doped. The source excites ions into a greater energy and will decay via spectral of stimulated emission which has a photon at the signal wavelength back to a lower energy level. The spontaneous emission (decay) can occur to the exited ions or even via non-radiative mechanism involving interactions with phonons of the glass matrix. The last two decay processes compete with stimulated emission, which decreases the efficiency of amplitude or intensity of electromagnetic amplification. The *amplification window* represents the range of wavelengths for which the amplifier results in an applicable gain. This is determined by the measurement of the glass structure of fiber optic or by spectroscopic properties of dopant ions and the wavelength and power of the electromagnetic source. Even though the transitions of electronic or an isolated ion are very well known, the wide band of the energy levels happens if the ions are interacted to the fiber optic. Therefore, the amplification window is also broadened. The broadening will be homogeneous (all ions exhibit the same broadened spectrum) and also it will be inhomogeneous (different ions in different glass locations exhibit different spectra). A relatively high-powered beam of electromagnetic source such as light is combined with the input signal by using a wavelength selective coupler (WSC). This input one and the excitation beam have to be of different wavelengths significantly. The mixed electromagnetics or polychromatics or laser will be guided into a resonator of fiber with erbium ions subject to the fiber core. The high-powered electromagnetics of light beam excites the dopants ions to the higher-energy state. If photons of signal at a particular resonant wavelength from the beam source meet the excited erbium atoms, the erbium atoms will surrender several of their energy to the signal and go back to their lower-energy state. The main point is that the erbium surrenders up its energy in the form of additional photons with the similar phase and direction as the signal being multiplied and amplified. Thus, the signal is amplified along the direction of transmission. This is not unusual—if an atom "lases," it always surrenders its energy in the same direction and phase as the incoming beam source. Therefore, a whole additional signal source is guided in the similar fiber mode as the incoming signal. Usually, an isolator is placed at the output port to overcome reflections going back from the attached optical fiber. As reflections disrupt amplifier operation, in the extreme case, it will cause the amplifier to become a laser. The ED (erbium-doped) compound has a great gain.

2.2. Semiconductor optical amplifier

SOA is an amplifier of small size using a semiconductor to provide the gain medium [4] and pump electronically. It operates as the same as standard semiconductor lasers and is packaged in tiny size as "butterfly" design. In addition to their tiny size, they are low cost. SOA suffers from a quantity drawbacks making it not suitable for wide applications. In special case, it gives relatively low gain (<15 dB), has a low saturated output power (<13 dBm), and has relatively high NF. SOA has quick response time providing the operation to near the saturation level. They suffer from signal distortion for single channel setup and noise as effect of cross-gain modulation such as WDM operation and can suit for single channel booster where they do not require high gain or high output power. SOA has the same formation to Fabry-Pérot laser diodes but with anti-reflection elements at the end faces. Nowadays, the designs include antireflective coatings and tilted waveguide and window regions which can decrease end-face reflection <0.001%. Because it produces power losses from the resonator which can be higher than the gain, it prevents the amplifier from the source of laser. There are two kinds of SOA. One region is a laser diode having a Fabry-Pérot, and the second one is a tapered geometry to decrease the value power density on the output facet. SOA is particularly made from III-V compound periodic system such as InGaAs/ InP, AlGaAs/GaAs, InAlGaAs/ InP, and InGaAsP/InP, though any direct band gap semiconductors such as II-VI will conceivably be applied. These components are usually used for amplifier in telecommunication systems and technology such a fiber-pigtailed components, operating at signal wavelengths between 0.85 and 1.6 μm and generating gains of up to 30 dB [5].

2.3. Raman amplifier

Raman amplifier (RA) amplifies signal by stimulated Raman scattering (SRS). SRS is a device having a process of electromagnetic wave scattered by ions or molecule compound from a lower state to a higher state of wavelength source. Sufficient great power source at a lower state which stimulated scattering may happen if data signal with a higher wavelength state is multiplied and amplified by Raman's from the source. SRS actually represents a nonlinear interaction between higher and lower wavelength. It can take place in optical waveguide. The efficiency of SRS is low for most fibers having high pump power particularly 1 W to obtain useful signal gain. Generally, RA cannot compete to EDFAs as depicted in **Figure 4**.

Raman amplification provides two unique benefits to other amplification telecommunication and technologies. This amplification wavelength band can be tailored by changing the source of wavelengths. It can be obtained at wavelengths that are not supported by competing technologies. The Raman amplification can be also achieved within the propagation wave in the optical fiber itself, enabling a distributed Raman amplification (DRA). In this mechanism, a high source power is launched into the optical fiber (from the output end) to amplify the wave signal to the fiber optics. Because the gain happens along the optical fiber cable, DRA prevents the wave signal from being damped or attenuated to very low powers, improving the SNR of information signal. RA is also always used with EDFAs to deal with the ultra-low

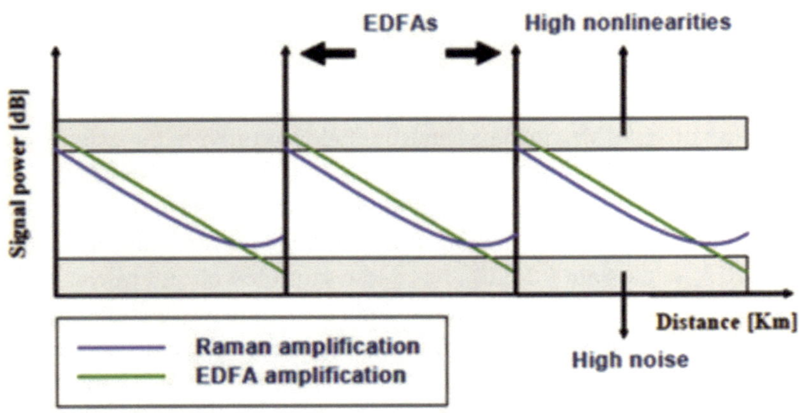

Figure 4. Signal power for Raman and EDFA.

NF-combined amplifiers. These are beneficial to many usages in communication, for example, ultra-long links spanning by order of 10^3 km, the long links with no in-line amplifiers, or very high bit-rate (40/100 Gb/s) links.

It is not like the EDFA and SOA; the effect of amplification is achieved by nonlinear factors between the optical signal and a laser source within the optical waveguide. There are two kinds of RA, i.e., distributed and lumped one. The former is the transmission fiber used as the gain medium by multiplexing a source wavelength with signal wavelength, while latter one utilizes a dedicated, shorter length of optical waveguide to provide amplification. Particularly, a lumped RA with highly nonlinear fiber having a small core is applied to enhance the interaction to signals and source wavelengths and thereby decreases the length of optical fiber required. The laser source may be combined to the fiber of transmission signal with the same direction (codirectional pumping), on the other direction (contra-directional pumping), or both. Contra-directional pumping source is often used as the noise transfer to the source pump to the signal decreased. Source power of RA is greater than that of the EDFA, >500 mW being required to achieve useful levels of gain in a distributed amplifier. In lumped amplifiers, the pump light can be safely contained to avoid safety implications of high optical powers, may use over 1 W. The principal advantage of Raman amplification is its ability to amplify and distribute the signal within the waveguide, by increasing the length of spans between amplifier and regeneration sites. The amplification bandwidth represents the source wavelengths used so that the amplification can be provided over wider, and different, regions than it is possible with other amplifier which depends upon dopants and optical component design to introduce the amplification "window."

Other advantages of RA are as follows. Firstly, its gain is available in fiber, providing a cost-effective means of upgrading of the terminal ends. Secondly, the Raman gain is non-resonant, that gain is available over the whole transparency area of the fiber approximately 0.3–2 μm. Thirdly, by organizing the source of wavelengths, the gain may be tailored such as the multiple source lines can be utilized in order to enhance the bandwidth, and also the source distribution describes the gain flatness. The benefit to Raman amplifier is a broadband amplifier with a bandwidth relatively >5 THz, this result gain is reasonably flat over a wide wavelength range. But, the challenges of Raman amplifiers prevent their earlier adoption. Firstly, if one compares to the EDFAs, RA has relatively less pumping efficiency at lower-level signal power. Even though it has a disadvantage, this lack of pump efficiency becomes gain clamping readily in RA. Secondly, RA requires a longer gain of optical fiber. On the other hand, this disadvantage can be mitigated by mixing gain and the dispersion compensation in a single fiber. Thirdly, it has a fast response time, which gives rise to new sources of noise. Finally, there are concerns of nonlinear penalty in the amplifier for the WDM signal channels. Amplifier parameters will allow the amplification of a weak signal impulse in a non-centrosymmetric nonlinear medium. On the other hand, the amplifiers are mostly used in telecommunication application and technology. This kind finds its main application in expanding the frequency tunability of ultrafast solid-state lasers. For a noncollinear interaction geometry, its optical parameters are suitable for extremely wide bandwidths for amplification.

3. Design and model of SOA and FRA circuit

The suitable amplifier is one way to deal with the effects of linear and nonlinear disturbances as well as maximize the working of optical transmission media. Generally the optical amplifier consists of fiber Raman amplifier (FRA), erbium-doped fiber amplifier (EDFA), and semiconductor optical amplifier (SOA). SOA is designed in the form of quantum-dot SOA network as linear network and bulk SOA as nonlinear network [2]. Then, it is known that SOA has a high nonlinear nature, low power consumption, fast operating speed, and can easily be used in photonic systems [6–9].

In SOA type amplifier, the gain can be calculated using the following equation:

$$g_m = A_g(N - N_0) \tag{1}$$

where g_m = material amplifier, A_g = coefficient of derivative gain, N = carrier density, N_o = carrier density at the point of transparency.

$$g_t = \Gamma g_m - \alpha \tag{2}$$

where g_t = coefficient of amplifier, Γ = optical confinement factor, α = effective loss coefficient.

$$G = \exp[g_t z] \tag{3}$$

where G = magnitude of gain (dB), z = length of optical fiber (dB).

Then, Bromage introduced the RA used in fiber-optic communication systems [10]. The gain on this amplifier can be calculated using the equation as follows:

$$G = 10\log(\exp[gPL]) \tag{4}$$

$$g = 2\gamma\rho\,\mathrm{Im}(\chi_{1111}[\omega_p - \omega_s]) \tag{5}$$

$$\gamma = \frac{2\pi n_2}{\lambda A_{eff}} \tag{6}$$

where G = magnitude of gain (dB), P = power pump (Watt), L = length of optical fiber (m), n_2 = nonlinear refractive index (m^2. W^{-1}), γ = nonlinear phase change (rad), A_{eff} = effective surface (m^2), λ = wavelength signal (m), g = Raman gain coefficient, ρ = nonlinear polarization fraction, $X_{1111}(\omega_p - \omega_s)$ = Raman's susceptibility.

Both amplifiers show that the type of SOA more considered the carrier density and the material factor, whereas FRA more considered the frequency characteristics and wave nonlinear conditions. However, both amplifiers are very dependent on the media passed by the signal. In order to investigate the performance of SOA and FRA, bit error rate (BER) and Q-factor are two parameters used to measure their characteristics.

http://dx.doi.org/10.5772/intechopen.79941

BER and Q-factor are the most important factors that limiting the transmission distance in optical communication system. In order to transmit signals over long distances, it is necessary to have a low BER and high Q-factor within the fiber. The optical amplifier in the fiber represents the optical signals to be directly amplified optically without any conversion. The BER is an indication of how often data is retransmitted due to an error. Too high BER may indicate that a slower data rate will actually improve overall transmission time for a given amount of transmitted data because the BER may be decreased, lowering the quantity of packets that has to be present. In BER, the quantity of measured bits is incorrect before error correction, divided by the total amount of transferred bits (including redundant error codes). Usually, the BER is larger than the information data of it. The information of BER is influenced by the strength of the forward error correction program and code. There are kinds of BER occurring in optical communication circuit. It can be affected by transmission noise, interference, distortion, bit synchronization problems, attenuation, wireless multipath fading, etc. However, in both amplifiers, we consider the simple channel model and data source model.

Another factor is Q-factor, which explains the resonance performance of disturbance that is particularly shown by an underdamped harmonic oscillator. The driven cavity or resonators having high number of Q-factor will resonate with larger intensity, which is shown by amplitudes (at certain frequency). They have more tiny bandwidth range of frequencies around that frequency. They will resonate having frequencies that are defined as a bandwidth. The high value of Q-factor oscillators oscillates with more tiny range of frequencies and more stable condition. Q-factor unit is dimensionless describing how underdamped an oscillator is and characterizes a resonator's bandwidth relative to its center frequency.

The design of the network model will be simulated using OptiSystem version 11.1.0.53. In the model, the SOA and FRA optical amplifiers are coupled to the transmission amplifier network (in-line amplifier). **Figure 5** shows the design of model, optical fiber communication system.

3.1. Information source block

The information source block consists of two components: pseudorandom bit sequence (PRBS) and *non-return-to-zero pulse generator* (NRZ). PRBS functions to generate bits with specific patterns and speeds. Then the bit that has been generated by PRBS will be encoded using NRZ coding technique. NRZ coding technique has the advantage that is more resistant to noise and is not affected by the voltage level. **Figure 6** shows the planning drawing for the source of pulse information.

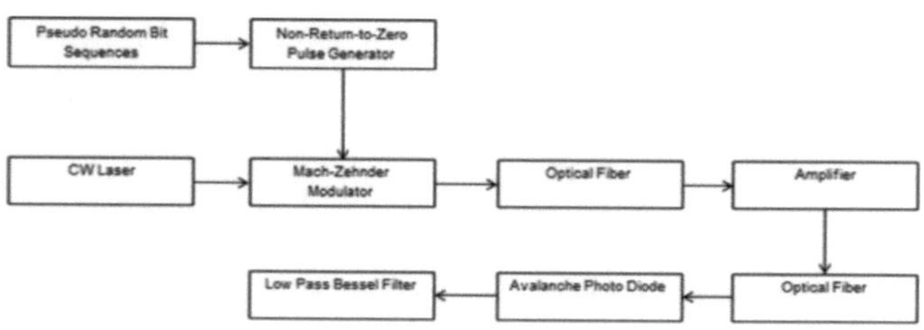

Figure 5. Model design with amplifier.

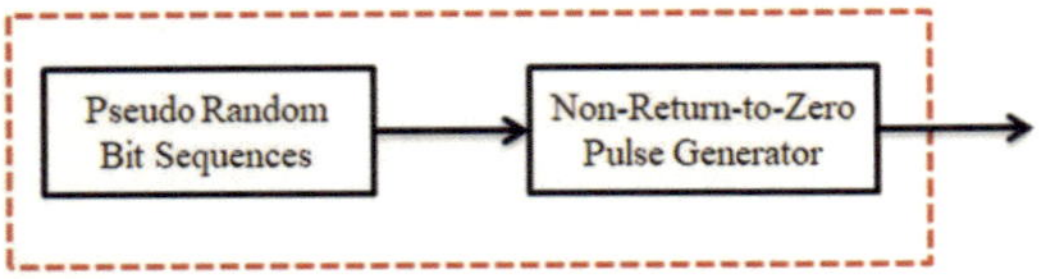

Figure 6. Information source block.

3.2. Transmitter block

The transmitter block (**Figure 7**) consists of two components: the laser and the modulator. The laser acts as a light signal generator on a network system. The type of laser used is a continuous wave (CW) laser. The modulator used is the Mach-Zehnder modulator (MZM) which will modulate the coded information signal with the output signal laser.

3.3. Transmission media block

The transmission medium (**Figure 8**) on this optical network uses single-mode optical fiber, because it has a wide bandwidth and a considerable range. In order for the transmitted signal to reach a considerable distance, it requires an optical amplifier, SOA and FRA. Type of TRD used is average power model amplifier (APA).

3.4. Receiver block

The receiver block consists of two components: a detector and a filter. The detector used is avalanche photodiode (APD) as shown in **Figure 9**, because it has a faster response and higher gain. The already converted information signal will be forwarded to the filter. The working principle of this filter passes a certain frequency and dampens other frequencies. The type of filter used is the *low-pass Bessel filter*.

The stages of this procedure begin with a preliminary simulation process that aims to determine the maximum transmission distance of signal propagation on the optical fiber without any gain. In the simulation process, it will iterate on the optical fiber, for 30 iterations, and each iteration is 10 km. Then, the determination of maximum transmission distance is demonstrated by using SOA and FRA. The working procedure of these two optical amplifiers can be seen in **Figures 10** and **11**. The length of fiber optics greatly affects the performance of a communication system. In determining the maximum transmission length, the parameters that

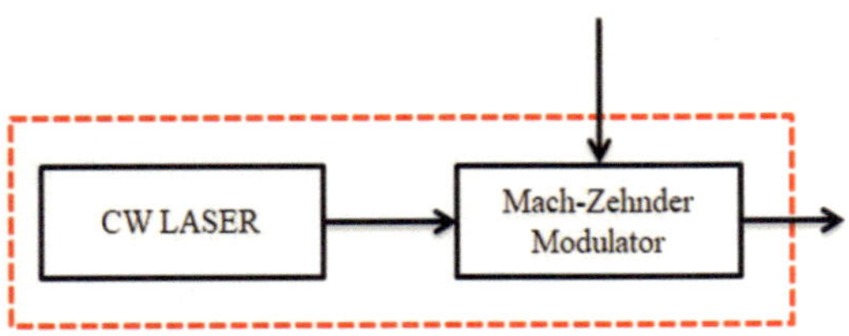

Figure 7. Transmitter block.

http://dx.doi.org/10.5772/intechopen.79941

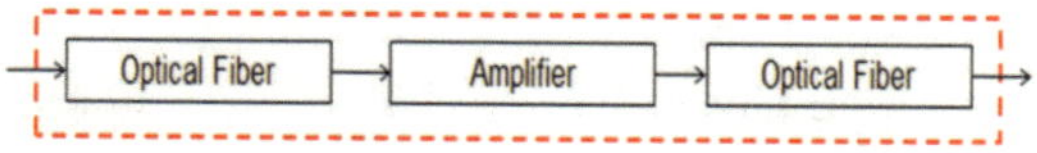

Figure 8. Transmission media block.

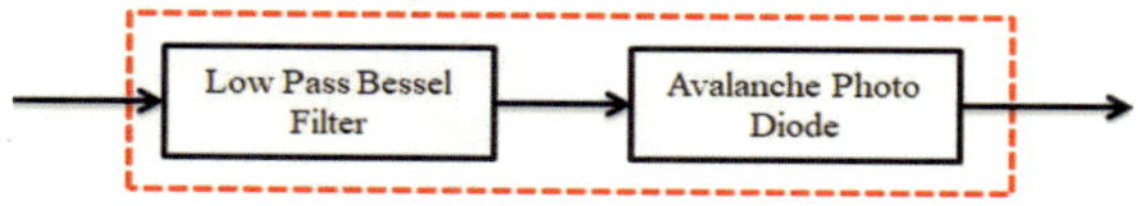

Figure 9. Receiver block.

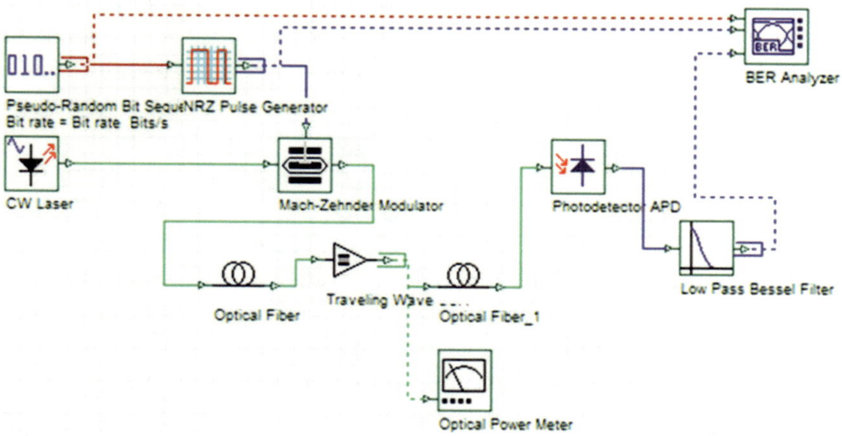

Figure 10. Optical fiber system scheme with SOA in-line amplifier.

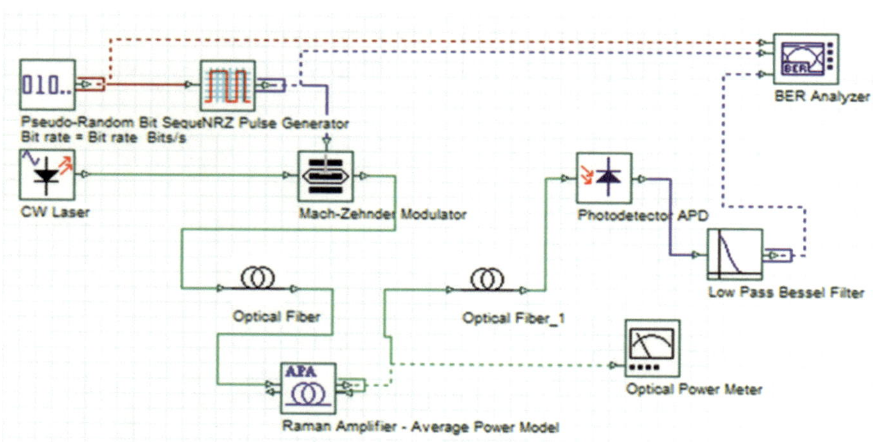

Figure 11. Optical fiber system scheme with FRA in-line amplifier.

play an important role are the bit error rate (BER) and Q-factor. According to the rules of the International Telecommunication Union (ITU-T G.691; ITU-T G.692; ITU-T G.693), the BER requirements for optical communication systems must be better than 10^{-12}, meaning that the minimum value of BER system should be smaller than 10^{-12}. Q-factor is a quality factor that will determine the quality of a link. In a fiber-optic communication system, the minimum size of a good Q-factor is 6. The power consumption of the amplifier will be measured using the optical power meter contained in the circuit. We will then see the influence of the wavelength on the maximum transmission distance of the system.

4. Propagation and amplification of SOA and FRA

The result of SOA is depicted in **Figure 12**. The BER can be discussed by applying a model and simulation using a computer. A propagation model and data source mode are simply considered; the BER can be calculated analytically as well. If the device for BER analysis is not available, OTDR can be applied to detect the wave losses through the OptiSystem software for detecting the BER. A schematic flowchart of **Figure 10** is depicted to this analysis. BER is found in SOA where 1350 nm wavelength with 1 mW input power is better than the others since it has higher energy than 1470 nm and 1560 nm, so that BER oscillation depends on energy. However, after about 150 km, BER value increases. It is not surprising when the distance is long then the error will come; this is due to attenuation of geometry length where it can operate either low- or high-energy sources corresponding to wavelength source. Even at 120 km, the highest BER is achieved for 1350 nm (highest energy). This is the weaknesses of SOA characteristics. Although these data are unknown source of loss factors, improving BER may be measured by choosing strong signal, a slow and robust modulation pattern, or line coding signal such as repetitive forward error correction program (**Figure 13**).

As well as BER of SOA, Q-factor of SOA goes down as the distance is increased. But, Q-factor for 1350 nm (highest energy) is even less decayed than the others. Although the decay trends are stable beginning from 80 km similar to a constant Q-factor, at 140 km, the energy source is not good enough to maintain the oscillation source; hence the decay goes down near linear including 1350 nm and keeps maintaining to reduce it slowly. This performance shows that at

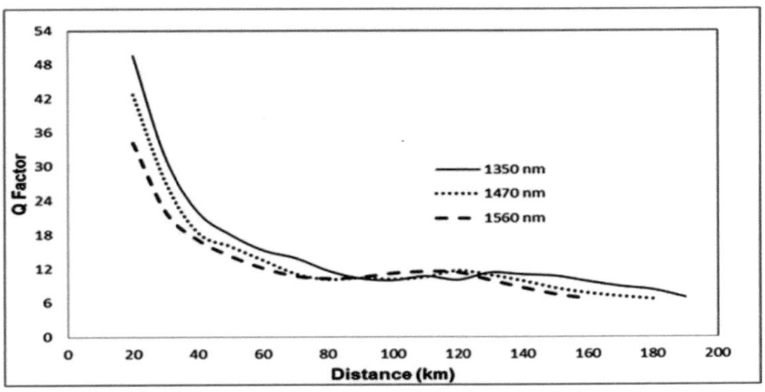

Figure 12. BER for SOA.

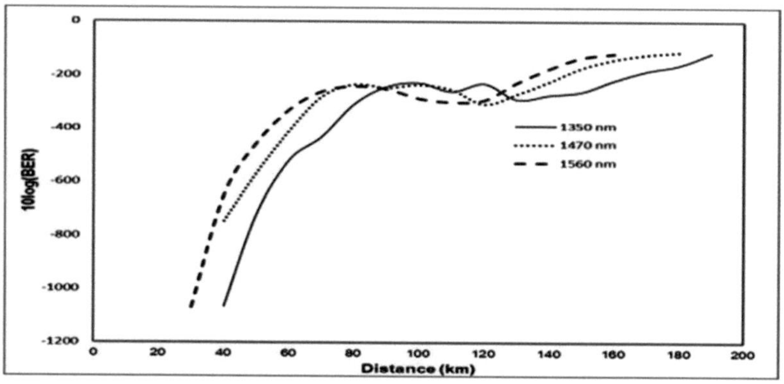

Figure 13. Q-factor of SOA.

wavelength of 1350 nm, the dispersion is more than the wavelength of 1560 nm, but Q-factor oscillation is low. Unlike SOA, FRA has good performance for both BER and Q-factor. The result of FRA for BER and Q-factor is depicted in **Figures 14** and **15**. BER is less fluctuated and more stable for higher energy of $E = hf$, where f is frequency source, h is Planck constant, and E is energy. From 60 to 140 km, BER is nearly constant for various wavelength sources; hence this BER is better than SOA. Q-factor is faster for a stable condition at higher energy at 80 km and continues after 160 km.

Figure 16 is an eye pattern diagram with no amplifier. It is generally seen that the amplitude and bit error rate differ greatly at the lower distances at (a) than (b). The weakness of the unfocused amplitude is due to the power and geometry of the far wave from the wave source. The red line facing below is BER, and the red line facing the top is Q-factor.

In **Figure 17**, both wavelengths at 160 km distance have a low Q-factor especially at low-wave energy. SOA function is very effective at a distance less than 100 km, but at the peak of 160 km, the wave amplitude is not focused anymore. Amplitude is affected by distance even if SOA is used.

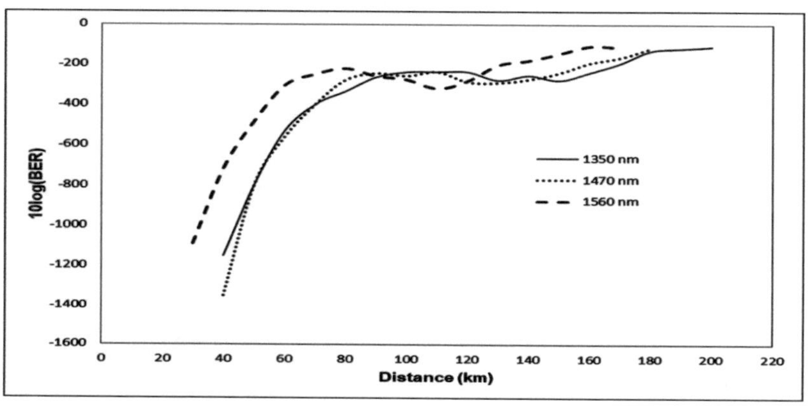

Figure 14. BER for FRA profile.

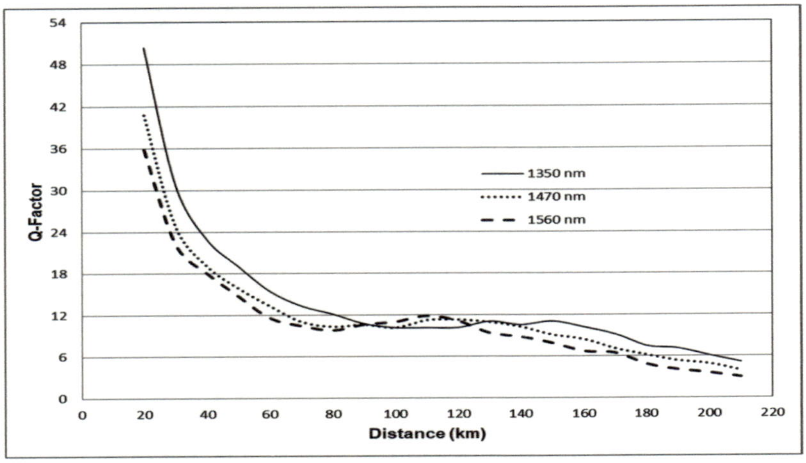

Figure 15. Q-factor of FRA profile for various energy.

Figure 18 is somewhat different than SOA. FRA has a more effective BER and Q-factor. At a distance of less than 90 km, the very sharp eye pattern at 1350 nm wavelength is almost equal to the 1560 nm wavelength. The value of FRA at a distance of 170 km is still more effective than on SOA values both at 1350 nm and at 1560 nm. However at 1560 nm, BER is more sharp as Q-factor as well. BER and Q-factor at 1560 are higher so that the amplifier function is weak especially at great distances.

4.1. Optical circuits without amplifier BER and Q-factor analysis

The length of the optical fiber used can affect the performance of a fiber-optic communication system. In determining the maximum transmission length, one of the parameters that play an important role is the amount of bit error rate (BER). The BER requirement for the optical communication system should be less than 10^{-12}. The first stage is a simulation process without using an optical amplifier to determine the maximum transmission length with laser wavelength variation. BER is shown in **Figure 19**.

Since the data obtained is in a very small order, then the data change in the form of logarithmic functions. The BER value for an optical source with a wavelength of 1350 nm is 2.12×10^{-12}

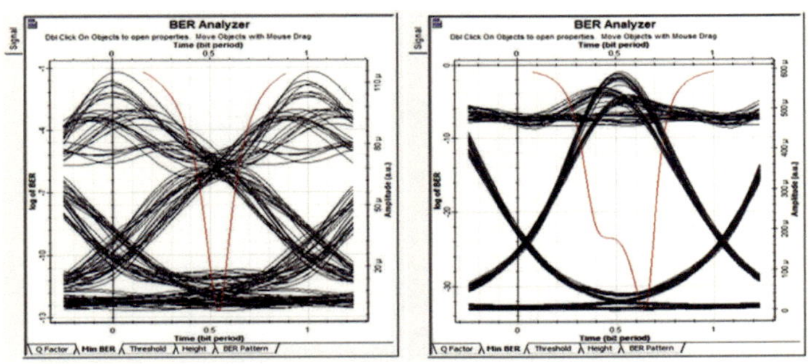

Figure 16. (a) 1350 nm, 85 km. (b) 1560 nm, 85 km.

http://dx.doi.org/10.5772/intechopen.79941

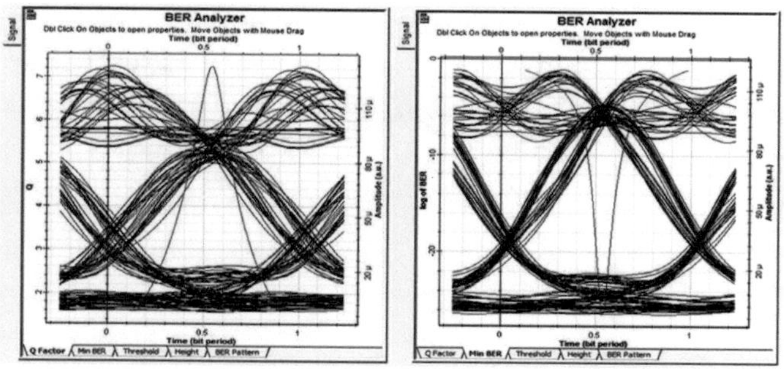

Figure 17. (a) SOA (BER and Q-factor) 1350 nm, 80 km. (b) SOA (BER, Q-factor) 1560 nm, 160 km.

or −116.74 dB at a distance of 95 km and 3.51×10^{-9} or −84.55 dB at a distance of 100 km. The BER value for an optical source with a wavelength of 1470 nm is 1.64×10^{-13} or −127.85 dB at a distance of 85 km and 1.66×10^{-9} or −87.80 dB at a distance of 90 km, whereas the BER value for an optical source with a wavelength of 1560 nm is 1.26×10^{-12} or −119 dB at a distance of 80 km and 3.56×10^{-9} or −84.49 dB at a distance of 85 km. So it can be concluded from Figure 4.1 that the maximum transmission distance of the fiber-optic communication system without the amplifier is 95 km for the 1350 nm wavelength, 85 km for the 1470 nm wavelength, and 80 km for the 1560 nm wavelength.

In addition to the BER value, Q-factor is one of the parameters used as a reference in determining the quality of the optical circuit. Under the rules of ITU (International Telecommunication Union) in ITU-T G.691; ITU-T G.692; ITU-T G.693, it is agreed that the minimum Q-factor value that must be possessed by an optical communication system is 6. This shows that a circuit can be categorized well if the circuit has a Q-factor above 6. In contrast, the circuit cannot be used if it has a number below that value.

Based on the simulation that has been executed, it obtains that the value of Q-factor at the source wavelength of 1350 nm is 6.59 at a distance of 95 km and 5.79 at a distance of 100 km. At the source wavelength of 1470 nm, the obtained value is 7.28 at a distance of 85 km and 5.91 at a distance of 90 km, while at the wavelength of 1560 nm, the found value is 6.32 at a

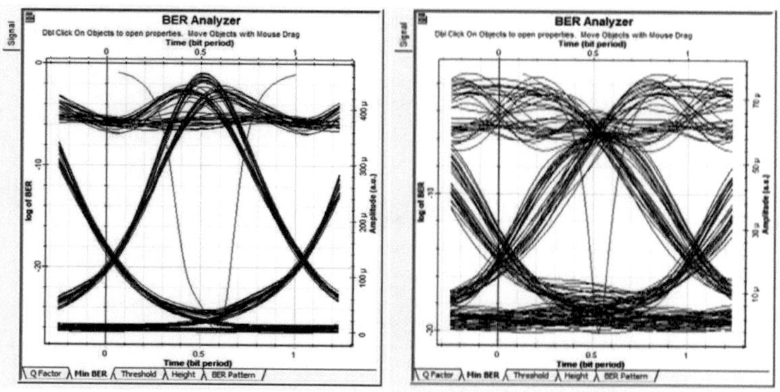

Figure 18. (a) Raman (BER and Q-factor) 1350 nm, 90 km. (b) Raman (BER and Q-factor) 1350 nm, 170 km.

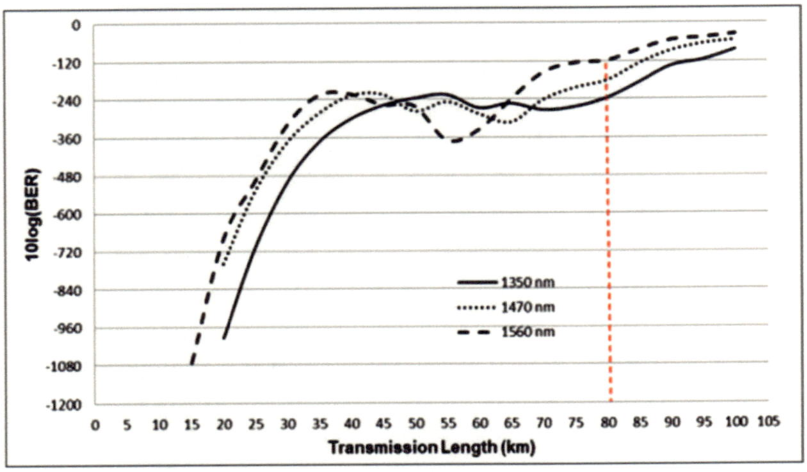

Figure 19. BER value to transmission length.

distance of 80 km and 5.79 at a distance of 85 km. So **Figure 20** corresponds to the BER data obtained where the maximum transmission distance at the source wavelength of 1350 nm is 95 km, 85 km at 1470 nm wavelength, and 80 km at 1560 nm wavelength.

4.2. SOA amplifier circuit BER and Q-factor

SOA is a type of amplifier that uses semiconductors to gain medium gain. SOA has a structure similar to the Fabry-Pérot laser diode, but it has an anti-reflection element on its surface. Unlike other amplifiers, SOA is electronically pumped directly through the current and does not require a separate laser pump. The working principle of SOA is similar to the laser, where in the active part of the semiconductor, the injection current will excite the electrons from the valence band to the conduction band. If there is light as an input signal, then the electron set will be stimulated to return to the valence band by emitting energy to gain reinforcement. Based on the simulation, SOA is depicted in **Figures 21** and **22**.

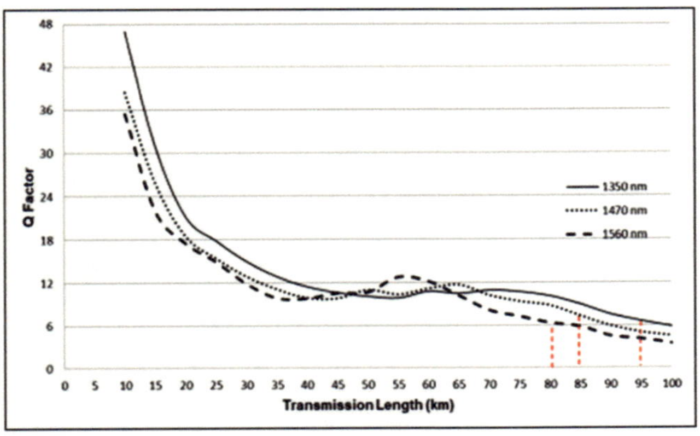

Figure 20. Q-factor on transmission length without amplifier of optical circuit.

http://dx.doi.org/10.5772/intechopen.79941

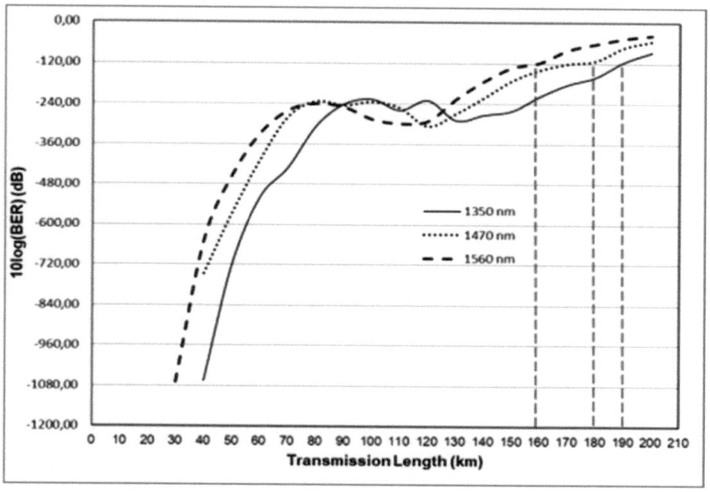

Figure 21. BER, transmitting on SOA circuit.

The BER value for an optical source with a wavelength of 1350 nm is 3.25×10^{-12} or −114.88 dB at 190 km and 2.31×10^{-9} or −86.36 dB at a distance of 200 km. The BER value for an optical source with a 1470 nm wavelength is 7.24×10^{-12} or −111.40 dB at a distance of 180 km and 5.63×10^{-8} or −72.49 dB at a distance of 190 km. The BER value for the optical source with a wavelength of 1560 nm is 1.85×10^{-12} or −117.33 dB at a distance of 160 km and 9.51×10^{-9} or −80.2 dB at a distance of 170 km. So it can be concluded from the graph that the maximum transmission distance of the fiber-optic communication amplifier SOA system is 190 km for the wavelength of 1350 nm, 180 km for the 1470 nm wavelength, and 160 km for the 1560 nm wavelength.

The Q-factor value (**Figure 22**) at the source wavelength of 1350 nm is 6.87 at a distance of 190 km and 5.86 at a distance of 200 km. At the source wavelength of 1470 nm, the obtained

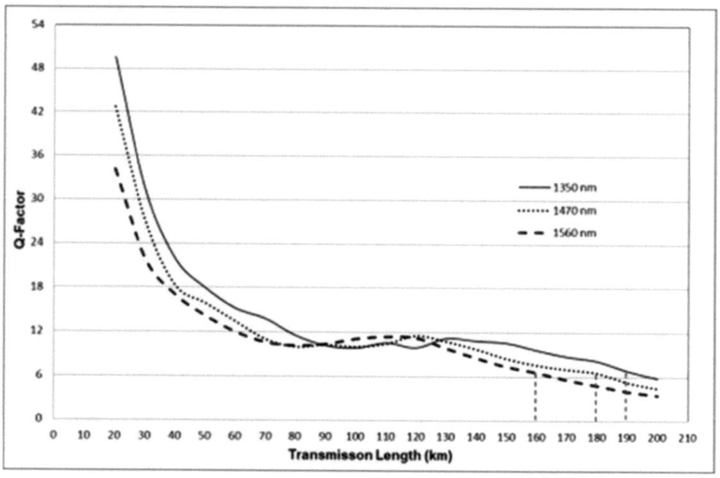

Figure 22. Q-factor of transmission length in SOA circuit.

value is 6.58 at a distance of 180 km and 5.30 at a distance of 190 km, while at the wavelength of 1560 nm, the found value is 6.61 at a distance of 160 km and 5.62 at a distance of 170 km. So this result corresponds to the BER data obtained where the maximum transmission distance at the source wavelength of 1350 nm is 190 km, 180 km at 1470 nm wavelength, and 160 km at a 1560 nm wavelength.

4.3. RFA circuit: BER and Q-factor

RA works based on the principle of scattering Raman (Raman scattering). This amplifier does not use a special medium/fiber for strengthening but uses only its transmission media. The characteristics of RA include:

- The strengthening mechanism uses stimulated Raman scattering (SRS).
- Effectively SRS deprives the energy of shorter wavelengths and gives it to longer wavelengths.

When a monochromatic light engulfs or crashes into a particle, there will be a certain interaction between the light and the particles it has hit. Light will be reflected, absorbed/refracted, or scattered. If scattering causes wavelength changes, then this phenomenon is called Raman scattering producing higher power.

The RA is an additional component of the development of the EDFA optical amplifier. Raman launches high-power laser into the optical waveguide in the opposite direction of the source signal. The photon injection amplifies the optical signal where it is needed almost at all over long distances. Reinforcement Raman can make signal boosters more than 10 dB, where skipping for longer distances. Also it allows optical network to achieve transmission speed up to 40 Gbits/s.

The nonlinear effect will appear in the fiber transmission which is the result of signal amplification if the optical signal is pumped by the wavelength and power is released into the fiber. Based on the simulation, FRA is depicted in **Figures 23** and **24**.

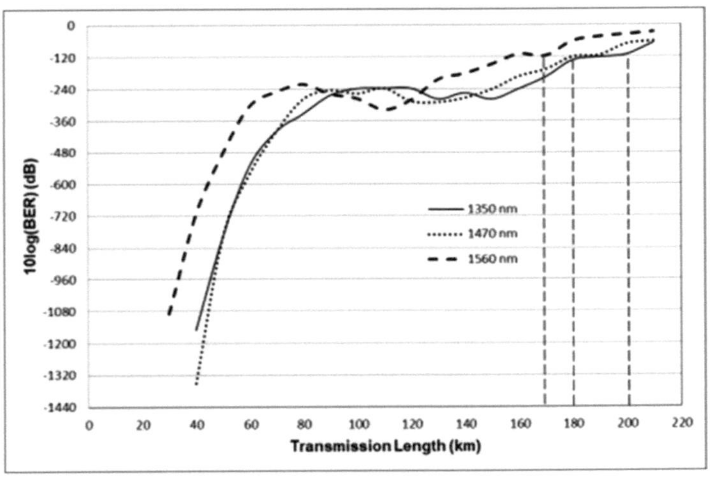

Figure 23. Graph of BER value to transmission length on FRA circuit.

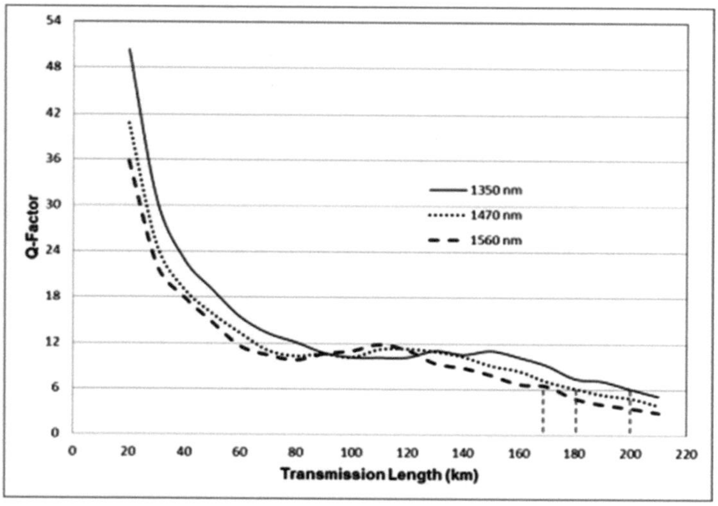

Figure 24. Q-factor of transmission length on the FRA circuit.

The BER value for an optical source with a wavelength of 1350 nm is 6.98 × 10^{-12} or −111.56 dB at a distance of 200 km and 1.62 × 10^{-7} or −67.90 dB at a distance of 210 km. The BER value for an optical source with a 1470 nm wavelength is 4.01 × 10^{-12} or −113.97 dB at a distance of 180 km and 5.73 × 10^{-8} or −72.42 dB at a distance of 190 km. The BER value for an optical source with a wavelength of 1560 nm is 2.94 × 10^{-12} or −115.32 dB at a distance of 170 km and 7.11 × 10^{-7} or −61.48 dB at a distance of 180 km. So it can be concluded that the maximum transmission distance of the fiber-optic communication amplifier FRA system is 200 km for 1350 nm wavelength, 180 km for 1470 nm wavelength, and 170 km for 1560 nm wavelength.

The Q-factor value in **Figure 24** at the source wavelength of 1350 nm is 6.06 at a distance of 200 km and 5.11 at a distance of 210 km. At the source wavelength of 1470 nm, the obtained value is 6.14 at a distance of 180 km and 5.30 at a distance of 190 km, while at the wavelength of 1560 nm, the found value is 6.42 at a distance of 170 km and 4.82 at a distance of 180 km. So this result corresponds to the BER data obtained where the maximum transmission distance at the source wavelength of 1350 nm is 200 km, 180 km at the 1470 nm wavelength, and 170 km at the 1560 nm wavelength.

4.4. Comparison between BER and Q-factor without amplifier SOA and FRA

Based on **Figures 25** and **26**, it can be seen at the stance the SOA reinforcement system is 180 km. But the BER value in the SOA amplifier circuit is larger, and the Q-factor is smaller than the FRA amplifier circuit. While in the circuit without the amplifier, the maximum transmission distance is only worth 90 km.

Based on **Figures 27** and **28**, at the 1350 nm source wavelength, the FRA amplifier optical circuit has a longer transmission distance than the SOA system, where the maximum distance on the FRA amplifier circuit is 200 km while the maximum distance on the SOA circuit is only

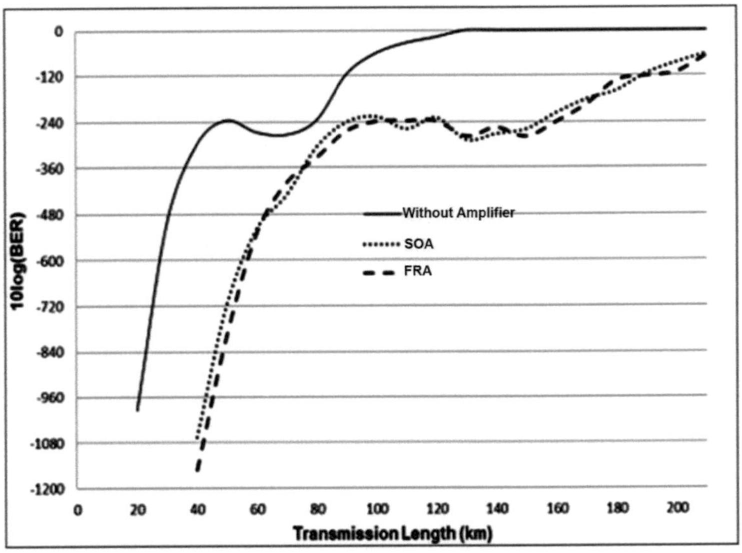

Figure 25. BER value over transmission length at wavelength of 1470 nm.

190 km. While in the circuit without the amplifier, the maximum transmission distance is only worth 90 km. This proves the role of the optical amplifier used so that the signal can propagate further when compared to the circuit without amplifier.

Based on **Figures 29** and **30** it can be seen at the largest source wavelength of 1560 nm, the TRA amplifier optical circuit has a longer transmission distance than the SOA system, where the maximum distance on the FRA amplifier circuit is 170 km while the maximum distance in the SOA circuit is only 160 km. While in the circuit without the amplifier, the maximum transmission distance is only worth 80 km.

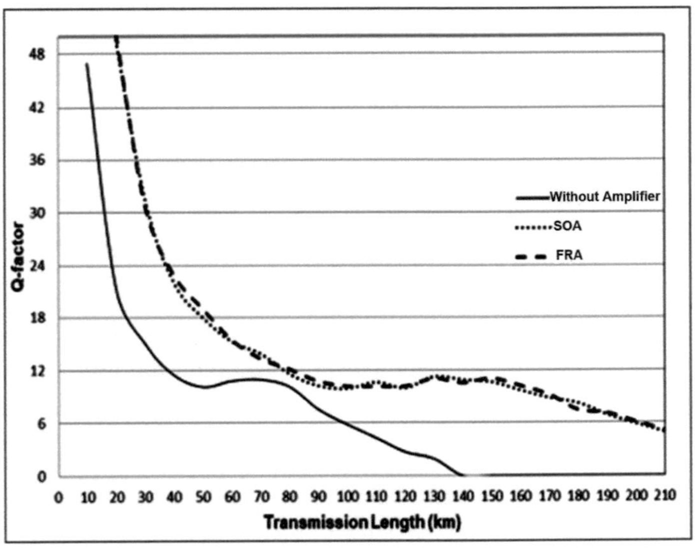

Figure 26. Q-factor to transmission distance at wavelength 1470 nm.

http://dx.doi.org/10.5772/intechopen.79941

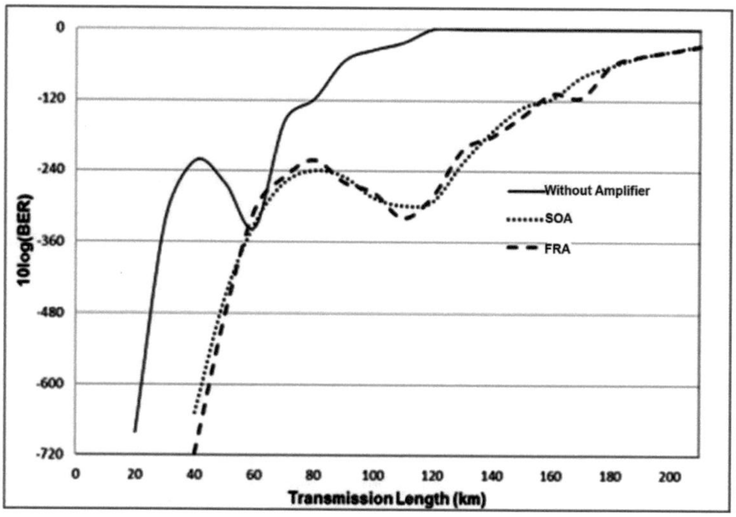

Figure 27. BER to transmission over wavelength at wavelength 1350 nm.

4.5. SOA and FRA: BER and Q-factor

The result of SOA of BER can be analyzed using computer simulations. When a simple transmission model and data source mode are considered, the BER can also be calculated analytically. In the absence of device for BER analysis, OTDR has been used for detecting signal losses in optical fiber and the OptiSystem software for analyzing the BER. The circuit diagram is used to do this analysis. BER is found in SOA where 1350 nm wavelength with 1 mW input power is better than the others since it has higher energy than 1470 and 1560 nm, so that BER oscillation depends on energy. However, after about 150 km, BER value increases. It is not surprising when the distance is long then the error will come; this is due to attenuation of

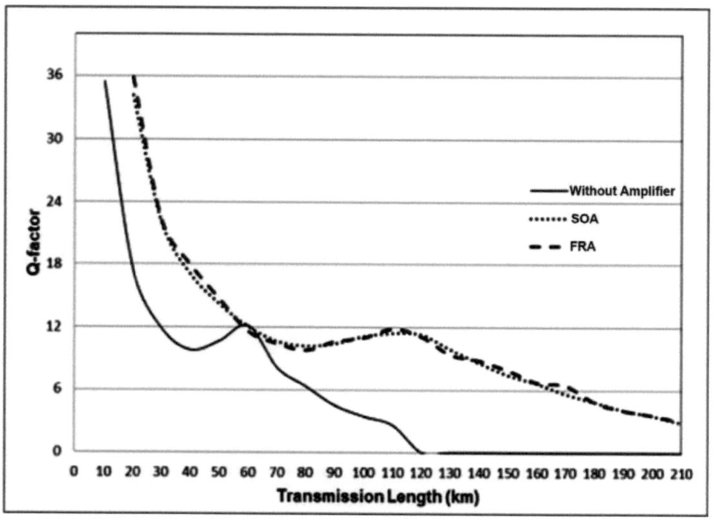

Figure 28. Q-factor over transmission length for wavelength 1350 nm.

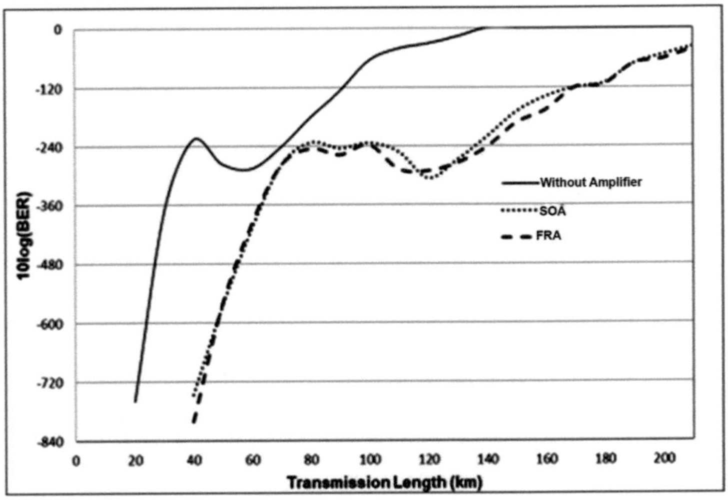

Figure 29. BER value over transmission length at wavelength 1560 nm.

geometry length where it can operate either low- or high-energy sources corresponding to wavelength source. Even at 120 km, the highest BER is achieved for 1350 nm (high energy). This is the weaknesses of SOA characteristics.

Although these data are unknown source of loss factors, improving BER can be detected by choosing strong signal strength, a slow and robust modulation scheme, or line coding scheme or using coding schemes such as redundant forward error correction codes. As well as BER of SOA, Q-factor of SOA goes down as a distance is increased. Q-factor for 1350 nm is even less decayed than the others, although the decay trends are stable beginning from 80 km similar to a constant Q-factor. At 140 km the energy source is not good enough to maintain the oscillation source; the decay goes down near linear for 1350 nm and keeps maintaining to reduce it slowly.

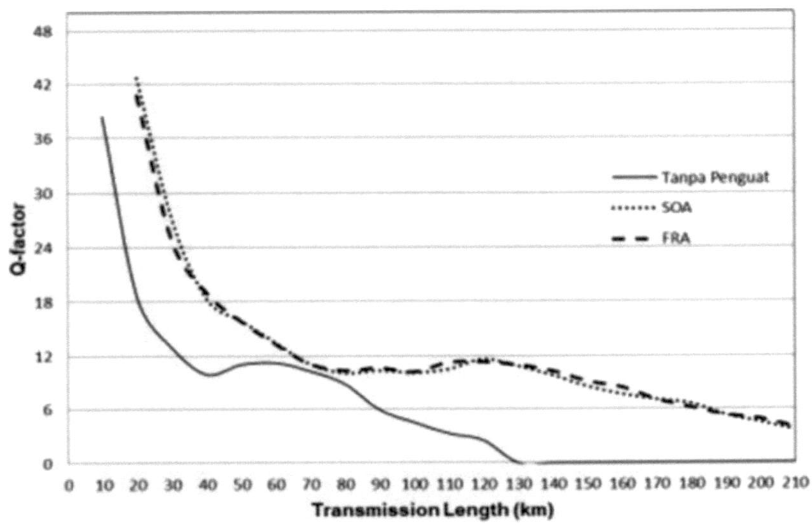

Figure 30. Q-factor to transmission length at wavelength 1560 nm.

Wavelength source (nm)	Transmission length (km)	Amplifier	Power input (dBm)	Power output (dBm)	Power consumption (dBm)
1350	100	FRA	0	−43.533	43.533
		SOA	0	−41.737	41.737
	190	FRA	0	−61.302	61.302
		SOA	0	−59.592	59.592
1470	100	FRA	0	−43.565	43.565
		SOA	0	−41.622	41,622
	180	FRA	0	−59.499	59.499
		SOA	0	−57.880	57.880
1560	100	FRA	0	−43.752	43.752
		SOA	0	−41.808	41.808
	160	FRA	0	−55.740	55.740
		SOA	0	−53.794	53.794

Table 1. Power consumption to FRA than SOA.

Unlike SOA, FRA has good performance for both BER and Q-factor. BER is less fluctuated and more stable for higher energy of $E = hf$, where f is frequency source, h is Planck constant, and E is energy. From 60 to 140 km, BER is nearly constant for various wavelength sources; hence, this BER is better than BER of SOA. Q-factor is faster for a stable condition at higher energy at 80 km and continues after 160 km. This performance shows that at wavelength of 1350 nm, the dispersion is more than the wavelength of 1560 nm, but Q-factor oscillation is low.

4.6. Power consumption

The measured power consumption is the power consumption in the FRA circuit and the SOA circuit. The input power used in both circuit types is 1 mW or 0 dBm. This input power comes from the laser, and the output power is measured on the detector device. The power measurement uses an optical power meter and an electrical power meter at the output that can calculate the signal power passing through which the device is placed. Power consumption is obtained by calculating the input power difference with output power. From **Table 1** it can be seen at wavelengths of 1350, 1470, and 1560 nm for in-line amplifier implementation, the power consumption of the SOA is smaller than that of the FRA circuit. The SOA has slightly more energy efficient when compared to the FRA requiring a pumping laser so that the lost power is greater.

5. Conclusion

Although the optical amplifier can maintain the signal along the trajectory of waveguide, several amplifiers still have weaknesses. Both SOA and FRA have advantages and disadvantages. Using the simulation application, both amplifiers are successfully designed and compared by in-line amplifiers. The results described that the transmission distance of the FRA is much farther than the SOA shown by BER and Q-factor. However, this FRA system has higher power consumption when compared to the SOA system.

Author details

Toto Saktioto* and Roby Ikhsan

*Address all correspondence to: saktioto@ieee.org

Department of Physics, Faculty of Mathematics and Natural Sciences, Universitas Riau, Pekanbaru, Indonesia

References

[1] Finisar White Paper. Introduction to Optical Amplifiers. Finisar Corporation. Sunnyvale, CA. 2012

[2] Karimah ZN, Hambali A, Suwandi. Analisis Perbandingan Kinerja Mach-Zehnder berdasarkan Ragam Format Modulasi pada Jaringan FTTH. Jurnal ELKOMIKA. 2017;**5**(1): 73-92

[3] Leuthold J, Bonk R, Vallaitis T, Marculescu A, Freude W, Meuer C, et al. Linear and nonlinear semiconductor optical amplifiers. In: Conference on Optical Fiber communication (OFC/NFOEC) Collocated National Fiber Optic Engineers Conference. San Diego: IEEE Xplore, Digital Library; 2010

[4] Bromage J. Raman amplification for fiber communications systems. IEEE Journal of Lightwave Technology. 2004;**22**(1):79-93

[5] Connolly MJ. Semiconductor Optical Amplifiers. Boston, MA: Springer-Verlag; 2002. ISBN: 978-0-7923-7657-6

[6] Sun H, Wang Q, Dong H, Dutta NK. XOR performance of a quantum dot semiconductor optical amplifier based Mach-Zehnder interferometer. Optics Express. 2005;**13**(6):1892-1899. DOI: 10.1364/OPEX.13.001892

[7] Hamie A, Sharaiha A, Guegan M, Pucel B. All-optical logic NOR gate using two-cascaded semiconductor optical amplifiers. IEEE Photonics Technology Letters. 2002;**14**(10):1439-1441. DOI: 10.1109/LPT.2002.802426

[8] Kanellos GT, Petrantonakis D, Tsiokos D, Bakopoulos P, Zakynthinos P, Pleros N, et al. All-optical 3R burst-mode reception at 40 Gb/s using four integrated MZI switches. Journal of Lightwave Technology. 2007;**25**(1):184-192

[9] Dong J, Zhang X, Fu S, Xu J, Shum P, Huang D. Ultrafast all-optical signal processing based on single semiconductor optical amplifier. IEEE Journal of Selected Topics in Quantum Electronics. 2008;**14**(3). DOI: 770-778. DOI: 10.1109/JSTQE.2008.916248

[10] Ghosh B, Mukhopadhyay S. All-optical wavelength encoded NAND and NOR operations exploiting semiconductor optical amplifier based Mach-Zehnder interferometer wavelength converter and phase conjugation system. Optics and Photonics Letters. 2011; **4**(2):1-9. DOI: 10.1142/S1793528811000172

Benefits and Challenges of Internet of Things for Telecommunication Networks

Asaad Ahmed Gad-Elrab Ahmed

Additional information is available at the end of the chapter

http://dx.doi.org/10.5772/intechopen.81891

Abstract

Recently, Internet of things (IoTs) has become the main issue in designing monitoring systems such as smart environments, smart cars, and smart wearable devices. IoTs has transformed the life of people to be more adaptable and intelligent. For example, in a healthcare monitoring system, using smart devices will improve the performance of doctors, nurses, patients, and the healthcare industry. The IoTs revolution is known as the fourth industrial revolution and would change the way humans interact with machines and lead the way to a high-technology machine-to-machine interaction. In fact, almost every device around us would be connected to Internet, collecting and exchanging data with other devices on the cloud. In this chapter, we will introduce the benefits of IoTs on telecommunication networks and its challenges to give a complete overview for researchers to know how to improve our life and society by building smart IoTs systems.

Keywords: IoTs, smart things, smart environments, green IoT, Security and privacy, big IoT data

1. Overview of IoT

In recent decades, due to the developments in wireless and computer technologies, processors and sensors have been embedded into a lot of objects, which are used in our life. To build and design a real smart environment, these advancements are supported by huge developments in many research and industrial areas such as ubiquitous computing, wireless mobile communications, portable appliances and devices, wireless sensor networking, machine learning-based decision-making, agent technologies, IPv6 support, and human computer interfaces. A smart environment has sensor-enabled devices working collaboratively to build a small connected world for making the lives of people more comfortable and adaptable. The term smart refers to the ability to autonomously obtain and apply knowledge, and the term environment refers to the surroundings. Therefore, a smart environment can be adapted by obtaining knowledge and applying it according to its users' requirements to improve their experience of that environment. In addition, the interconnection among different smart objects can enhance their functional capabilities [1]. In this context, IPv6 plays a vital role because of several features, including scalability in the case of billions of connected devices, better security mechanisms, and the elimination of network address translation (NAT) barriers. The "Internet of Things" (IoT) concept was first coined by Kevin Ashton, where smart objects are connected with the Internet.

Nowadays, IoT is receiving attention in many fields such as transport, agriculture, industry, and healthcare [2, 3]. Cisco reports that 50 billion devices and objects will be connected to the Internet by 2020. Also, the Internet of Things (IoT) will contribute $117 billion to the IoT-based healthcare industry and $1.9 trillion to the global economy according to Gartner and Forbes. In addition, according to Automotive News, the number of cars connected to the Internet worldwide will increase from 23 million in 2013 to 152 million in 2020. According to another report from Navigant Research, the number of installed smart meters around the world will grow to 1.1 billion by 2022. The prediction of such significant growth shows that IoT will become the umbrella of modern societies to realize the vision of smart environments. A lot of research efforts have been developed to integrate IoT with smart environments. To enable the user for monitoring the environment remotely or from remote sites, the integration of IoT with a smart environment is needed to extend the capabilities of smart objects. Based on the application requirements, IoT can be integrated with different smart environments. So, IoT-based smart environments can generally be classified into the following areas: (a) smart homes, (b) smart buildings, (c) smart cities, (d) smart grid, (e) smart health, (f) smart transportation, (g) smart industry, and (h) smart agriculture. **Figure 1** illustrates the IoT-based smart environments.

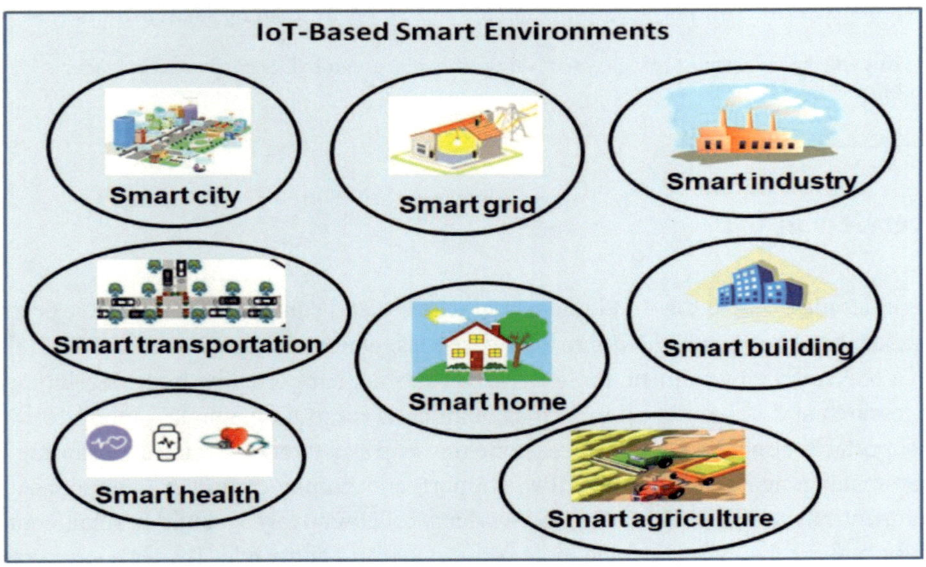

Figure 1. IoT-based smart environments.

2. Challenges of IoT

There are many open challenges that have been described by various researchers including those related to power supply, enabling a complex sensing environment, evolving architecture, multiple connectivity options, complexity of IoT, security of information exchange within IoT, and privacy [4–6]. Due to the lack of a clear and widely accepted business model that can engage investments to encourage the deployment of these technologies, there is difficulty in the adoption of the IoT paradigm [3].

To a certain extent, the above-mentioned challenges can be met, with the aid of a variety of wireless and wired connectivity options, such as radio frequency identification (RFID), near-field communication (NFC), Bluetooth, and Wi-Fi. These connectivity options are categorized into three broad types considering their geographical area coverage, that is, personal area network (PAN), local area network (LAN), and wide area network (WAN) [7]. **Figure 2** shows this categorization. The existing Wi-Fi networks should be modified to attain a wider coverage and to support mesh networks [8]. In addition, the confirmation on communication pathway of IoT is very important to understand the information exchange within IoT. It uses various standards, techniques, and protocols to disseminate information.

It is essential to support device-to-device (D2D), device-to-server (D2S), and server-to-server communications (S2S) to facilitate information sharing within the IoT [7, 9]. There are multiple standards and protocols involved with IoT communication. Some of these standards and

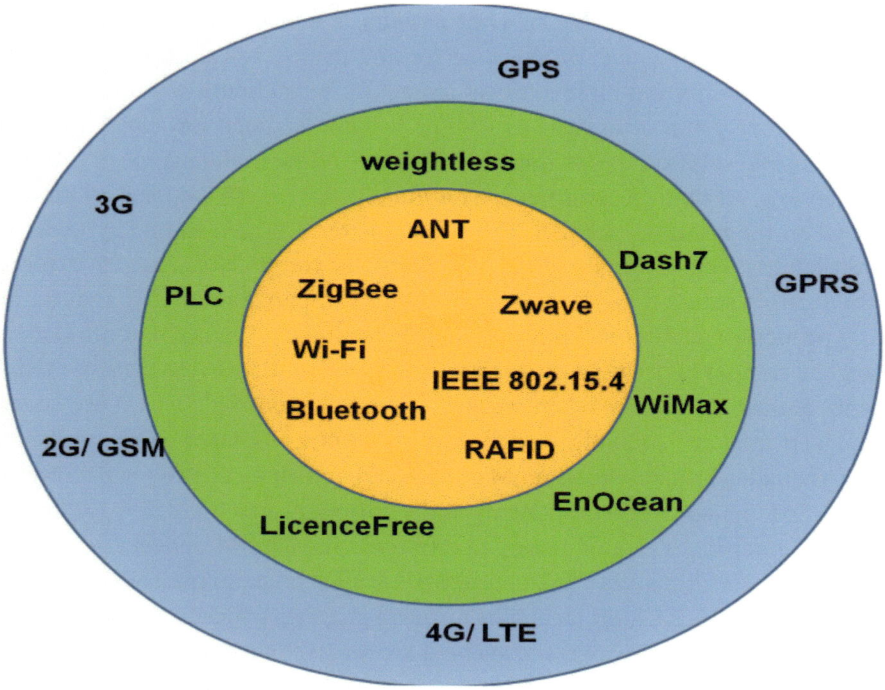

Figure 2. IoT communication technologies [7].

protocols take a higher priority, such as Internet Protocol version 4 (IPv4), Internet Protocol version 6 (IPv6), IPv6 over Low-Power Wireless Personal Area Network (6LoWPAN), User Datagram Protocol (UDP) Constrained Application Protocol (CoAP), and Transmission Control Protocol (TCP). However, UDP is advantageous and cost-effective, due to its smaller size and performance according to constrained device developers [10]. To find a model for arranging these protocols into constrained and unconstrained stacks according to the TCP/IP network layer architecture, some efforts were made. The unconstrained stack contains Hypertext Transfer Protocol (HTTP), common standards Extensible Markup Language (XML), and IPv4, whereas the constrained stack contains Efficient XML Interchange (EXI), CoAP, and 6LoWPAN which are protocols with similar functionality but the complexity is reduced significantly [3]. In real life, the IoT has been rapidly developed and deployed with the enormous contribution from companies and research centers [11]. However, IEEE 802.11, IEEE 802.3, and IEEE 802.15.4 are the most common standards related to IoT [10], and the Internet Engineering Task Force (IETF) protocol suite has a vital contribution toward IoT for determining the challenges for IoT [12]. So, recently IoTs are widely accepted for using in practical application scenarios. Matrices are available to measure the cost, processing speed, and communication speed. However, there are few studies on application layer protocols and performance of 6LoWPAN [13, 14], IPv6 routing protocol for low power and lossy networks (RPL) [15–17], and IEEE 802.15.4 [18]; a complete evaluation of IoT has not taken place until now. Hence, this gap needs to be filled up in near future, considering a holistic view of IoT.

In this section, common major challenges of IoT and its future directions will be introduced. These challenges are *performance, availability, reliability, security and privacy, scalability, precision, interoperability, compatibility, Big IoT Data, mobility,* and *investment*. IoT is used to facilitate information and data anywhere, at any time for any person based on his request [19]. So, to realize IoT, availability is a highly critical issue. The IoT network requires the high availability guarantee of physical devices as well as IoT applications for achieving high availability. The feasible solution to this issue is using redundant maintenance of programs and hardware devices, so that the program or redundant device can be used to perform load balancing when the failure exists [20]. There are situations where simplicity is disclosed to achieve availability, even though redundancy increases complexity. Thus, to achieve availability, the feasible solution is redundant hardware components. In [20], two redundancy models are proposed: passive and active redundancy models. The active redundancy model performed bad compared to the passive redundancy model. Also, in the passive model, spare components are activated only when the primary component fails and these components will be at sleep mode or partially loaded during the other times. The reference provided claims a mathematical model based on Markov chain, which estimates availability and reliability. Since IoT depends on components and performance of involving technologies, its performance cannot be evaluated using a simple mechanism. Moreover, the other factors that influence the performance of IoT are network traffic, huge amounts of data, and heavy reliance on the cloud [21]. Cloud facilitates resource sharing, which is a vital requirement of IoT environments. In addition, users are enabled access to the services irrespective of the location via an Internet connection with the convergence of cloud and IoT. The convergence of cloud and IoT follows IoT-centric cloud approach or cloud-based IoT approach. In either way,

http://dx.doi.org/10.5772/intechopen.81891

orchestration techniques, dynamic resource management, and dynamically offloading from clients/hosts to cloud are new challenges while overcoming existing individual challenges of IoT and cloud [22].

In critical applications, reliability is very important [23]. Reliability is not just sending reliable information, but being able to adapt to changing environmental conditions, be resistant to long-term usability and security problems [24]. In all aspects of software and hardware of IoT, reliability requires to be guaranteed. Attempts were made to explain clearly with the architecture considerations, the reliability consideration for transport, link, and application layers together [24]. Moreover, to describe and analyze reliability and cost-related properties of the service composition in IoT, a probabilistic approach was proposed [25].

Security and privacy are an essential requirement of most of the applications. In IoT, memory cards of a device have a limited storage capacity. So, only small amounts of data can be stored in them, and some of the data will be stored in other sites remotely. For these remote data, users do not want to disclose their information to others, so these data need high security and privacy. In terms of security, privacy, and governance rules, new technology is required to give users the ability to verify whether the company satisfies their service level agreement or not, dynamically. Therefore, they should adapt pertinent mechanisms for IoT, to meet the expected security level of a user. Privacy, communication, trusted sensing, computation, and digital forging are rarely addressed tasks in terms of security scope [26]. IoT does not adhere to common security standards and architecture; however, security has become a very important issue [27]. Traditional security architectures cannot fully satisfy the security requests of IoT, because of the existence of a huge number of heterogeneous devices that are connected together. As result, there is a large number of malware entry points, which increases vulnerability. By applying a biological immunology approach, a scheme has been proposed based on a dynamic defense security mechanism to alleviate these security issues in an IoT architecture [28]. In [26], attempts were done to secure IoT communications by ensuring the security of IoT devices. As the first step, computer-aided design (CAD) techniques have been proposed to design IoT devices, which are highly optimized in both energy and security. Importantly, compared to the expensive hardware-securing concepts proposed, CAD techniques can be used to implement strong and ample security with low cost. However, it is practically not in use until date.

In literature, there are several approaches for tackling the security issues in the current IoT paradigm. However, the authentication of devices and securing links in a dynamic mobility environment are still unresolved challenges. Thus, the authentication of IoT devices in real-world scenario still has unresolved issues. Researchers have warned of a realistic threat to the IoT community in the future in industries called "smart home hacking" to meet these challenges.

The increase in the number of smart devices and the advances of embedded technologies have increased the devices-to-person ratio up to 1.84 in 2010 [29]. In addition, the requirements from applications by a client increase over the time. So, the scalability of IoT, which is the ability to add more devices and services to IoT without degrading the Quality of service (QoS), must be considered. Due to the heterogeneity of devices and underlying technologies, scalability becomes a critical issue in IoT. To enable unified addition of new devices via a layered architecture, a distributed, interoperable architecture was proposed for IoT to address the scalability issues without degrading the QoS for the realization of IoT notion [30]. In [30], the authors propose three layers of IoT infrastructure: (1) virtual object layer (VOL), (2) composite virtual object layer (CVOL), and (3) service layer (SL). The base structure "IoT daemon" of the distributed architecture consists of the functionalities of the three layers which are object virtualization, service composition and execution, and service creation and management. Based on the processing power and memory, every object hosts its own IoT daemon. Various applications are unified by using the three layers of IoT daemon. VOL digitally represents the properties and functionalities of each object. However, to perform a task, multiple objects work in collaboration. Thus, during runtime, composite virtual object (CVO) is created as a mash-up of VOs corresponding to the task. To create a mash-up, potential VOs should be identified, which is done at the CVOL. With the aid of uniform representation of objects (virtual object (VO)), addition of new objects to the IoT network does not degrade QoS because all the devices are connected with distributed architecture. Also, there are scalability issues due to the increase of network elements (NEs) in the Internet. Compensating the scalability issues with a service-oriented path computation element (S-PCE) instead of conventional host-oriented PCE was proposed by Barbosa C. Souza et al. in [31]. The performance evaluation confirmed that the proposed model supports more network elements than host-oriented PCE by comparing results obtained and the logs of DNS servers [31].

Interoperability is another major concern with regard to IoT, since various types of devices are connected to each other via IoT. Hence, IoT should facilitate services to all these devices regardless of the type, as interoperability is a necessity. By adhering to standardized protocols, this can be achieved to a certain level at the network and application levels. Due to ambiguous interpretations of the same protocol, achieving interoperability is challenging. So, by avoiding such ambiguities, interoperability of IoT would become more realistic. In [32], a solution to address IoT resources using Web protocols via IoT hubs has been proposed. Thus, the interoperability challenges are reduced to data formats and presenting hub catalogues.

In IoT, most of the devices are mobile devices, which make the IoT scenario more complex. So, IoT applications need to deliver services by considering the mobility factor as well. There are available standard management protocols, that is Mobile IPv6 (network layer) and TCP migrate (transport layer), to facilitate mobility issues in IoT. However, these standards are too complex to be used in IoT nodes. For constrained devices in IoT, a CoAP-based mobility protocol (CoMP) was proposed [33]. Moreover, to ensure mobility, a group mobility management (GMM) mechanism is shown to be promising [34]. In this context, the leader machine does mobility management for the group of machines that are grouped according to mobility patterns.

Precision is another one of the most important challenges that need to be addressed in many smart IoT environments such as transportation, healthcare, and unmanned aerial vehicular networks, where devices and systems are connected globally. Compliance with stringent requirements becomes central to the health and safety of the machine operators, machines, and related businesses when dealing with precision machines that can fail if the timing is 1 ms. Available bandwidth and network latency are the key factors that can affect the precision of distributed IoT delay-sensitive mission-critical environments. Therefore, when deploying IoT in a smart environment, these parameters need to be considered. For example, longer network latencies can cause delays in applying car brakes and be very dangerous in the case of vehicle-to-vehicle communication in smart transportation environments. Successful IoT deployment in smart environments can be achieved by designing and developing high-precision systems.

Big data are another challenge in IoT because IoT is one of the largest sources of collecting large amounts of data. As mentioned earlier, by 2020 more than 50 billion devices will be connected with each other, which can lead to big data production. The performance of most IoT applications is based on the data management services. Therefore, due to big data generated by devices forming a smart IoT environment, managing the big IoT data in terms of processing, access, and storage requires highly scalable computing platforms that do not affect the performance of the application.

Compatibility is another challenge in an IoT-based smart environment, where various products are connected with each other. Due to the unavailability of a universal language, most of the products are unable to connect with each other and lead to compatibility issues. To connect devices with each other, collaboration among enterprises, such as LG, Philips, and Samsung, is required. People will be frustrated if these companies are not collaborated and they are only capable of using one brand, in this case. Therefore, the collaboration among these companies is demanded to obtain the infrastructure information of each product and design a universal coding language accordingly by developers. To ensure the success of IoT, a solution to compatibility issues is demanded.

Massive investment in IoT scenario is required for the investment decision to deploy an industrial IoT environment. In IoT, there is a difficulty for industries to adopt this technology where things are not open and interoperable in terms of hardware and software. Therefore, open and integrated hardware and software-based IoT solutions should be built for deployment in industries. In addition, instead of replacing these deployments with new systems, the solutions should be flexible enough for enabling industries to evolve and adapt to their changes. Expertise and investment are required for generating innovation within existing hardware and software architectures.

3. IoT-based smart environments

In this section, the state-of-the-art IoT-based smart systems are presented and categorized and classified according to application domain. The main categories are as follows: (a) smart homes, (b) smart building, (c) smart cities, (d) smart grid, (e) smart health, (f) smart transport, (g) smart industry, and (h) smart agriculture.

3.1. Smart homes

In [35], for detecting a fault in the software defined network (SDN)-based smart home environment, a cloud-based home solution was proposed. To find the faulty location in an

IoT-based smart home environment, four social relationships are defined, namely, IoTService, IoTphysical space, IoTNetwork, and IoTIoT. An SDN controller makes a status graph that contains information on each home IoT to resolve the dependencies by collecting information from the packets passing through SDN switches, and the stateless protocol is used by Web-based services, which are not made for long-term sessions.

3.2. Smart buildings

In terms of cost, accuracy, intrusiveness, and privacy, existing occupancy monitoring approaches were analyzed by Akkaya et al. in [36]. For improving the occupancy detection accuracy in a smart building, they used multi-modal data fusion. In the information fusion techniques, noisy measurements generated from IoT devices are filtered and occupancy status is predicted. To reduce the energy consumption of the smart building, they also investigated how occupancy monitoring techniques could be used with data fusion techniques. EUFP7 IoT is a project to devise authentication and authorization mechanisms for service access protection. To extend the security functionalities stated by the architectural reference model for EUFP7 IoT, the framework was proposed in [37]. In [37], the authors proposed this framework to utilize the available localization data and to implement the access control for services provided in smart building. The proposed framework is based on a service management platform which is a city explorer that implements the key security aspects.

3.3. Smart cities

For urban IoT, the authors in [3] presented a survey on the architectures, protocols, and enabling technologies. They describe link layer technologies, Web service-based IoT architecture, and devices suitable for the urban IoT architecture. To enable various IoT applications, a generic top-down IoT architecture for smart cities was proposed in [38]. The integrated information center run by the IoT service provider is the core element of this architecture. This information center is connected to a set of services, such as water, electrical energy, central gas supply, provided in smart cities. Several technologies that are essential for the realization of smart cities, such as IoT co-building, openness, and convergence, are facilitated by this architecture.

In [39], Al-Hader et al. proposed a five-level pyramid architecture for smart cities as shown in **Figure 3**. The bottom layer is the smart infrastructure layer including water, electronics, fire protection, natural gas, electronic communications, and network. The next layer is the smart database resources layer including database server, data resources, and databases. The next layer is the smart building management system layer including building automation, control network, and HVAC. The next layer is the smart interface layer including dashboard, common operational platform, and integrated Web services. The top layer is the smart city. Some of the major functionalities that can be included in smart cities are street lighting, maintenance, waste management, surveillance, building, and emergency health monitoring.

3.4. Smart grid

In [40], an IoT-based real-time monitoring system was proposed for power transmission lines to avoid disasters. In the proposed system, conductor galloping, wind deviation, conductor

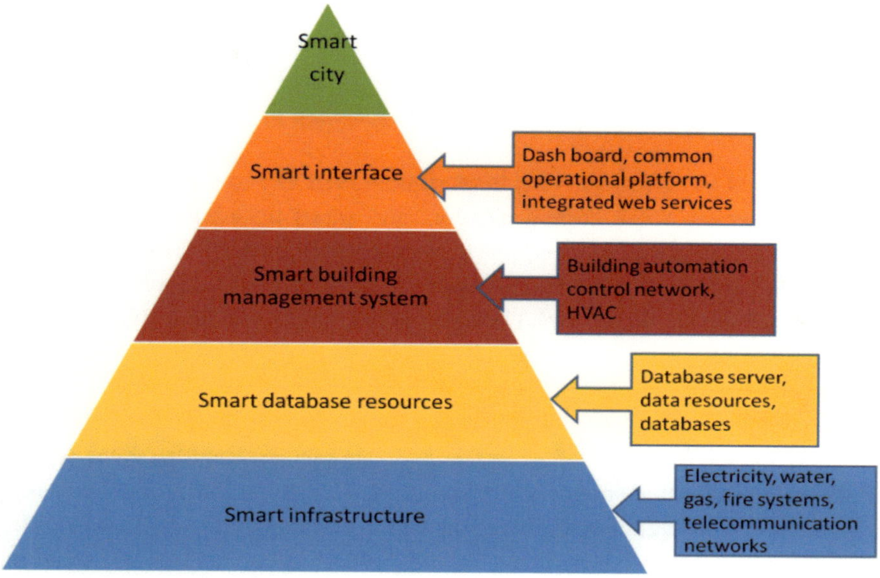

Figure 3. A pyramid architecture for smart cities [39].

temperature, icing, and tower leaning are visually displayed at the monitoring center. These parameters represent the power transmission lines and operational parameters of the tower. So, the system can implement real-time monitoring and early warnings of disaster for minimizing the damage of smart grid caused by natural disasters. In [41], IoT-based smart grid applications were classified into three types: (a) key equipment state monitoring, (b) information collection, and (c) smart grid control. It also describes the types and characteristics of IoT-based smart grids. As a result, a reference architecture for smart grid IoT based on the characteristics was proposed. There are three layers in this reference architecture: perception layer, transport layer, and application layer. For security protection of IoT-based smart grids, a secure access control system is proposed for ensuring that IoT-based smart grid devices can securely access the Internet.

3.5. Smart health

In [42], to monitor, collect, and transmit remote healthcare data, a system architecture based on IoT was proposed. To transfer data to a gateway, IEEE 802.15.4 standard was used and static and adaptive rule engines were developed as well. Through transmitting data based on important parameters extracted from the collected data, these two rules are involved in the decision-making process. As a result, these developed rule engines can minimize network traffic and save energy consumption. To solve issues such as reliability, interoperability, performance, energy efficiency, scalability, and security, the authors in [43] presented a smart e-Health gateway based on IoT. Based on taking responsibility of handling the sensor networks implemented in the remote healthcare center, this smart gateway can address these issues. The authors presented a case study called UTGATE for this smart e-Health gateway. Based on the achieved results from this case study, the smart e-Health gateway can provide services such as fast data processing, storage, and embedded data mining.

3.6. Smart transportation

The IoT can be used in all aspects of transportation such as geo services, collection of data related to passenger counting, communication, and smart ticketing. In [44], Eurotech provides IT solutions that can help in connecting every public transport element and use the technical tools to connect IT infrastructure with sensors and other devices. To enhance the traffic conditions in cities, the Kapsch Group in [45] investigated how Internet technologies can be leveraged.

3.7. Smart industry

In [46], the authors presented smart factory based on IoT architecture and defined issues such as optimized decision-making, flexibility, remote monitoring, and mass customization, with respect to energy management. By using the proposed mechanism, energy consumption is improved in a smart factory by incorporating energy data into production management.

3.8. Smart agriculture

Water utilization and irrigation can be improved by leveraging weather forecast and farm data, key trends and anomalies, and evapotranspiration index. Building IoT-based smart farming will enable farmers and growers to reduce waste and enhance productivity ranging from the number of journeys the farm vehicles have made to the quantity of fertilizer utilized. In IoT-based smart farming, with the help of sensors such as light, humidity, temperature, soil moisture sensors, a system is built for monitoring the crop field and automating the irrigation system. This system is highly efficient when compared with the conventional approach, and it gives farmers the ability to monitor the field conditions from anywhere.

4. Green IoT

Because of the increasing awareness of environmental issues all over the world, green IoT technology initiatives should be taken into consideration. The concept of greening IoT refers to the technologies that make the IoT environment more healthy in a friendly way by making use of facilities and storages that enable subscribers to gather, store, access, and manage various information. The enabling technologies for green IoT are called information and communication technologies (ICTs) [47]. ICTs can cause climate change in the world [48–52] because with the growing application of ICT much more energy has been consumed. The consideration for sustainability of ICTs has concentrated on data centers optimization through techniques of sharing infrastructure, which leads to increasing the energy efficiency, reducing CO_2 emissions and e-waste of material disposals [53]. Greening ICT is enabling technologies for green IoT, which includes green wireless sensor networks (GWSNs), green machine-to-machine communication (GM2M), green RFID, green data center (GDC) [5], green cloud computing (GCC), green Internet, and green communication network as shown in **Figure 4**. Therefore, green ICT technologies play an essential role in green IoT and provide many benefits to the society such as decreasing the energy used for designing, manufacturing, and distributing ICT devices and equipment.

Greening IoT is the practice of designing, manufacturing, disposing of computers, servers, and associated subsystems (i.e., monitors, printers, communications equipment, and storage devices) efficiently and more frequently but with reduced effect on the society and the environment [54]. The aim of using green IoT is to look for new resources and minimize IoT devices' negative impact on the health of humans and its disturbance to the environment. The main objective of greening IoT is to reduce pollution and Co_2 emission, exploit environmental conservation, and minimize the costs of things operating and power consumption [55–57]. Details about industrial emissions are analyzed and provided in [58]. These emissions influence environmental change in different regions and over time. Reducing the energy consumption of IoT devices is needed to make the environment healthier [59]. Due to the continuous development of green ICT technologies, green IoT provides a high possibility to support environmental sustainability and economic growth [57]. These valuable and emerging technologies make the world greener and smarter. Therefore, this section reviews the core of green IoT technologies that demonstrate efforts for constructing a green and smart world.

Green IoT consists of designing and leveraging aspects. Green IoT focuses on reducing IoT energy usage and CO_2 emissions, a necessity for building a smart world with the sustainability of intelligent everything. As shown in **Figure 5**, design elements of green IoT refer to developing computing devices, energy efficiency, communication protocols, and networking architectures [57].

The IoT element can be used to eliminate CO_2 emissions, reduce the pollutions and enhance the energy efficiency. Uddin et al. [60] introduced techniques for enhancing the energy efficiency and reducing CO_2 emission for enabling green information technology. Since M2M is equipped with sensors and communication add-ons, these devices can communicate with each other and sense the world. However, sensors will consume high power for executing the tasks. In networking, green IoT aims to identify the location of the relay and number of nodes which satisfy budget constraints and energy saving. To achieve a smart and sustainable world, green IoT plays a significant role in deploying IoT to reduce energy consumption [47], CO_2 emission [61] and pollution [61–63]; exploit environmental conservation [64];

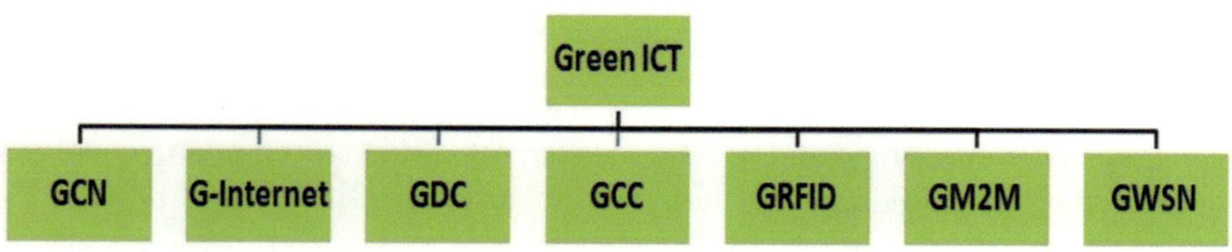

Figure 4. Green ICT technologies.

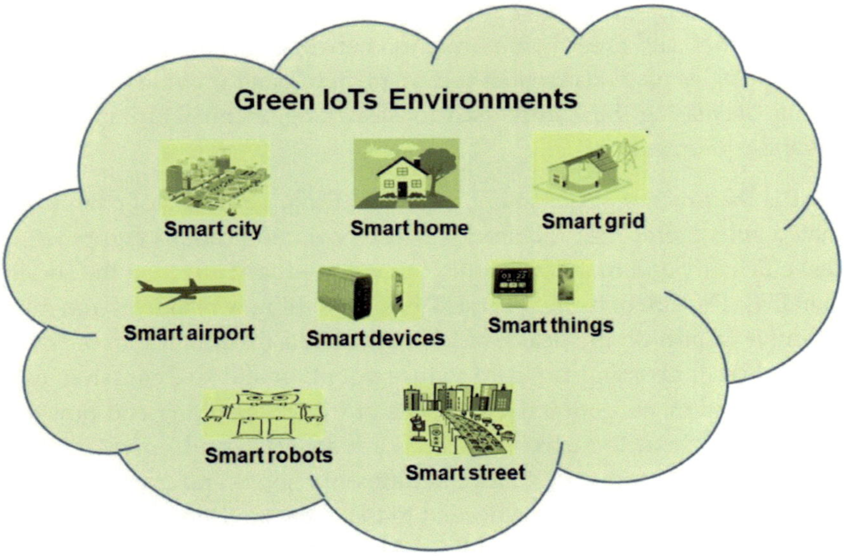

Figure 5. Green IoT environments.

and minimize power consumption [65]. Also, green IoT in [66] is defined as "the study and practice of designing, using, manufacturing, and disposing of servers, computers, and associated subsystems such as monitors, storage devices, printers, and communication network systems efficiently and effectively with minimal or no impact on the environment." There are three concepts for achieving green IoT, namely, design technologies, leverage technologies, and enabling technologies. Design technologies refer to the energy efficiency of devices, communication protocols, network architectures, and interconnections. Leverage technologies refer to cutting carbon emissions and enhancing energy efficiency. Due to green ICT technologies, green IoT has become more efficient through reducing energy, hazardous emissions, resources consumption, and pollution. Consequently, green IoT leads to preserving natural resources, minimizing technology's impact on the environment and human health, and reducing the cost significantly. Therefore, green IoT is indeed focusing on green manufacturing, green utilization, green design, and green disposal [67]. These issues are described as follows.

1. **Green use**: minimizing power consumption of computers and other information systems as well as using them in an environmentally sound manner.
2. **Green design**: designing energy efficient for green IoT sound components, computers, and servers, and cooling equipment.
3. **Green disposal**: refurbishing and reusing old computers and recycling unwanted computers and other electronic equipment.
4. **Green manufacturing**: producing electronic components and computers and other associated subsystems with minimal or no impact on the environment.

http://dx.doi.org/10.5772/intechopen.81891

5. Applications and services for IoT in smart environments

The integration of IoT with smart environments has brought about unprecedented opportunities. This section highlights the main opportunities offered by this environment.

5.1. Real-time information

In an IoT-based smart environment, organizations can collect data about processes and products for analysis in a real-time manner and provide the analyzed information to make appropriate decisions. Based on the decisions taken, the smart environment can rapidly adapt itself and improve operational efficiency that results in higher customer satisfaction.

5.2. Cost-effective cloud-based applications

Cost-effective, flexible, and secure cloud-based applications can transform a smart environment into a decision-making platform by collecting data from the environment and transferring them to the cloud through IoT. The key tasks performed in the cloud server are the analysis of these collected data, decision-making, and prediction of environment parameters.

5.3. New business models

IoT gives companies the ability to build new business models and revenue streams that can create many new business opportunities. IoT has the capability to change the way consumers and businesses follow the world. Therefore, consumers and businesses will require new services that can assist them to explore this ultra-connected, changing landscape. In addition, IoT can enable companies to create new revenue streams and services on top of traditional services, for example, vending machine vendors offering inventory management to those who supply the goods in the machine.

5.4. Intelligent operations

With rapid growth in IoT devices, the data produced by the IoT also grow exponentially. The management of such huge amounts of data will be a challenge in terms of performance. Designing intelligent cloud operation management solutions that can ensure the working of a cloud infrastructure at an optimal level will also be necessary.

6. Future of IoT

Due to the integration of novel concepts as well as the adaption of existing technologies, IoT is still evolving. Thereby, it supports the development of more competitive, realistic, and advanced IoT-based applications. The development of IoT applications based on the client requirements evolves according to the requirements of the users. Moreover, many organizations and interest groups are prepared to standardize IoT-related technologies to ensure more effective and secure applications.

The bright future of green IoT will change our future environment to become healthy, green, very high QoS, and sustainable socially, environmentally, and economically. Recently, the most exciting areas have focused on greening things such as green design and implementations, green communication and networking, integrated RFIDs and sensor networks, green IoT services and applications, energy-saving strategies, mobility and network management, smart objects, the cooperation of homogeneous and heterogeneous networks, and green localization. The following research fields need to be researched to develop optimal and efficient solutions for greening IoT:

1. There is a need for unmanned aerial vehicle (UAV) to replace a massive number of IoT devices, especially in agriculture, traffic and monitoring, which will help to reduce power consumption and pollution. UAV is a promising technology that will lead to green IoT with low cost and high efficiency.

2. Transmission data from the sensor to the mobile cloud must be more useful. Sensor-cloud is integrating the wireless sensor network and mobile cloud. It is a very hot and promising technology for greening IoT. A green social network such as a service (SNaaS) may investigate the energy efficiency of the system, service, WSN, and cloud management.

3. M2M communication plays a critical role to reduce energy use and hazardous emissions. Smart machines must be smarter to enable automated systems. Machine automation delay must be minimized in case of traffic and taking necessary and immediate action.

4. Design Green IoT may be introduced from two perspectives which are achieving excellent performance and high QoS. Finding suitable techniques for enhancing QoS parameters (i.e., bandwidth, delay, and throughput) will contribute effectively and efficiently to greening IoT.

5. While going toward greening IoT, it will be required to use less energy, looking for new resources, minimizing IoT's negative impact on the health of humans and disturbance to the environment. Then, green IoT can contribute significantly to sustainable, smart, and green environment.

6. To achieve energy-balancing for supporting green communication between IoT devices, the radio frequency energy harvest should be taken into consideration.

7. More research is needed to develop the design of IoT devices which helps to reduce CO_2 emission and energy usage. The critical task for smart and green environmental life is saving energy and decreasing the CO_2 emission.

7. Conclusion

In this chapter, the overview and benefits of IoT on telecommunication networks and their challenges were introduced to know how to improve our life and society by building smart IoT systems. In addition, the concept of green IoT and its related services and applications were described in detail. Finally, many research fields, which are needed to develop optimal and efficient solutions for greening IoT, were introduced.

Acknowledgements

This research was supported by the Department of Mathematics, Faculty of Science, Al-Azhar University, Cairo, Egypt. In addition, it was partially supported by King Abdul-Aziz University, Jeddah, Saudi Arabia. I thank both of them for providing guidance to finish this research. I also thank IntechOpen Limited for giving the opportunity for publishing this research work as a book chapter in Telecommunications Networks.

Author details

Asaad Ahmed Gad-Elrab Ahmed[1,2]*

*Address all correspondence to: asaadgad@azhar.edu.eg and aaahmad4@kau.edu.sa

1 King Abdul-Aziz University, Jeddah, Saudi Arabia

2 Department of Mathematics, Faculty of Science, Al-Azhar University, Cairo, Egypt

References

[1] Hayajneh T, Almashaqbeh G, Ullah S, Vasilakos AV. A survey of wireless technologies coexistence in WBAN: Analysis and open research issues. Wireless Networks. 2014; **20**(8):2165-2199

[2] Almashaqbeh G, Hayajneh T, Vasilakos AV, Mohd BJ. QoS-aware health monitoring system using cloud-based WBANs. Journal of Medical Systems. 2014;**38**(10):1-20

[3] Zanella A, Bui N, Castellani A, Vangelista L, Zorzi M. Internet of things for smart cities. IEEE Internet of Things Journal. 2014;**1**(1):22-32

[4] Atzori L, Iera A, Morabito G. The Internet of things: A survey. Computer Networks. 2010; **54**(15):2787-2805

[5] Gluhak A, Krco S, Nati M, Pfisterer D, Mitton N, Razafindralambo T. A survey on facilities for experimental Internet of things research. IEEE Communications Magazine. 2011; **49**(11):58-67

[6] Texas Instrument Organization. The Internet of things: Opportunities & challenges [Online]. 2014. Available from: http://www.ti.com/ww/en/internet_of_things/pdf/14-09-17-IoTforCap.pdf

[7] Internet of Things Technologies. Postscapes [Online]. Available from: http://postscapes.com/internet-of-things-technologies%20#communication

[8] Kasznik E. Internet of things: The third wave of revolution. World Intellect. Property Rev. [Online]. 2015. Available from: http://www.worldipreview.com/contributed-article/semiconductor-focus-the-third-wave-of-revolution

[9] Schneider S. Understanding the protocols behind the Internet of things. Electronic-design [Online]. 2013. Available from: http://electronicdesign.com/iot/understanding-protocols-behind-internet-things

[10] Internet of things protocols & standards. Postscapes [Online]. Available from: http://postscapes.com/internet-of things-protocols

[11] Ganchev I, Ji Z, O'Droma M. A generic IoT architecture for smart cities. In: ISSC 2014/CIICT 2014, Limerick; 2014

[12] Sheng Z, Yang S, Yu Y, Vasilakos A, McCann J, Leung K. A survey on the IETF protocol suite for the Internet of things: Standards, challenges, and opportunities. IEEE Wireless Communications. 2013;**20**(6):91-98

[13] Enjian B, Xiaokui Z. Performance evaluation of 6LoWPAN gateway used in actual network environment. In: International Conference on Control Engineering and Communication Technology (ICCECT), Liaoning; 2012

[14] Khoshdelniat R, Sinniah G, Bakar K, Shaharil M, Suryady Z, Sarwar U. Performance evaluation of IEEE802.15.4 6LoWPAN gateway. In: 17th Asia-Pacific Conference on Communications (APCC), Sabah; 2011

[15] Long N, De Caro N, Colitti W, Touhafi A, Steenhaut K. Comparative performance study of RPL in wireless sensor networks. In: IEEE 19th Symposium on Communications and Vehicular Technology in the Benelux (SCVT), Eindhoven; 2012

[16] Yushev A, Lehmann P, Sikora A. 6LoWPAN with RPL performance measurements in an Automated Physical Testbed. In: 2nd IEEE International Symposium on Wireless Systems within the Conferences on Intelligent Data Acquisition and Advanced Computing Systems, Offenburg; 2014

[17] Xie H, Zhang G, Su D, Wang P, Zeng F. Performance evaluation of RPL routing protocol in 6LoWPAN. In: 5th IEEE International Conference on Software Engineering and Service Science (ICSESS), Beijing; 2014

[18] Cheng X, Liang Q, He J. Analysis of IEEE802.15.4 network performance comprehensive evaluation and prediction. In: International Conference on Measurement, Information and Control (ICMIC), Harbin; 2013

[19] Marshal I, Alsaryraha O, Chung T, Yang C, Kuob W, Agrawal D. Choices for interaction with things on Internet and underlying issues. Ad Hoc Networks. 2015;**28**:68-90

[20] Macedo D, Guedes L, Silva I. A dependability evaluation for Internet of things incorporating redundancy aspects. In: ICNSC, Miami, FL; 2014

[21] Sevone. How will the Internet of things disrupt your performance monitoring strategy? – White paper [Online]. 2015. Available from: https://www.sevone.com/white-paper/how-will-internetthings-disrupt-your-performance-monitoring-strategy

[22] Biswas AR, Giaffreda R. IoT and cloud convergence: Opportunities and challenges. In: IEEE World Forum on Internet of Things (WF-IoT), Seoul; 2014

[23] Maalel N, Natalizio E, Bouabdallah A, Roux P, Kellil M. Reliability for emergency applications in Internet of things. In: IEEE International Conference on Distributed Computing in Sensor Systems (DCOSS), Cambridge, MA; 2013

[24] Kempf J, Arkko J, Beheshti N, Yedavalli K. Thoughts on reliability in the Internet of things [Online]. Available from: https://www.iab.org/wp-content/IAB-uploads/2011/03/Kempf.pdf

[25] Li L, Jin Z, Li G, Zheng L, Wei Q. Modeling and analyzing the reliability and cost of service composition in the IoT: A probabilistic approach. In: IEEE 19th International Conference on Web Services (ICWS), Honolulu, HI; 2012

[26] Xu T, Wendt J, Potkonjak M. Security of IoT systems: Design challenges and opportunities. In: IEEE/ACM International Conference on Computer-Aided Design (ICCAD), San Jose, CA; 2014

[27] Al-Fuqaha A, Guizani M, Mohammadi M, Aledhari M, Ayyash M. Internet of things: A survey on enabling technologies, protocols and applications. IEEE Communication Surveys and Tutorials. 2015;**17**(4):2347-2376

[28] Liu C, Zhang Y, Zhang H. A novel approach to IoT security based on immunology. In: 2013 9th International Conference on Computational Intelligence and Security (CIS), Leshan; 2013

[29] EvansD.TheInternetofthings–ciscoWhitepaper[Online].2011.Availablefrom:http://www.iotsworldcongress.com/documents/4643185/3e968a44-2d12-4b73-9691-17ec508ff67b

[30] Sarkar C, Nambi S, Prasad R, Rahim A. A scalable distributed architecture towards unifying IoT applications. In: IEEE World Forum on Internet of Things (WF-IoT), Seoul; 2014

[31] Barbosa V, Souza C, Masip-Bruin X, Marin-Tordera E, Ramirez W, Sanchez-Lopez S. Towards the scalability of a service-oriented PCE architecture for IoT scenarios. In: 20th European Conference on Networks and Optical Communications – (NOC), London; 2015

[32] Ishaq I, Carels D, Teklemariam G, Hoebeke J, Vanden Abeele F, De Poorter E, et al. IETF standardization in the field of the Internet of things (IoT): A survey. Journal of Sensor and Actuator Networks. 2013;**2**(2):235-287

[33] Chun SM, Park JT. Mobile CoAP for IoT mobility management. In: 2015 12th Annual IEEE Consumer Communications and Networking Conference (CCNC), Las Vegas, NV; 2015

[34] Fu H-L, Lin P, Yue H, Huang G-M, Lee C-P. Group mobility management for large-scale machine-to-machine mobile networking. IEEE Transactions on Vehicular Technology. 2013;**63**(3):1296-1305

[35] Kim Y, Lee Y. Automatic generation of social relationships between Internet of things in smart home using SDN-based home cloud. In: IEEE 29th International Conference

on Advanced Information Networking and Applications Workshops (WAINA); 2015. pp. 662-667

[36] Akkaya K, Guvenc I, Aygun R, Pala N, Kadri A. IoT-based occupancy monitoring techniques for energy-efficient smart buildings. In: IEEE Wireless Communications and Networking Conference Workshops (WCNCW). IEEE; 2015. pp. 58-63

[37] Herńandez-Ramos JL, Moreno MV, Bernabè JB, Carrillo DG, Skarmeta AF. Safir: Secure access framework for IoT-enabled services on smart buildings. Journal of Computer and System Sciences. 2014

[38] Ganchev I, Ji Z, O'Droma M. A generic IoT architecture for smart cities. In: 25th IET Irish Signals & Systems Conference 2014 and 2014 China-Ireland International Conference on Information and Communications Technologies (ISSC'14/CIICT'14). IET; 2014. p. 196199

[39] Al-Hader M, Rodzi A, Sharif AR, Ahmad N. Smart city components architecture. In: International Conference on Computational Intelligence, Modelling and Simulation, Brno; 2009

[40] Ou Q, Zhen Y, Li X, Zhang Y, Zeng L. Application of Internet of things in smart grid power transmission. In: Third FTRA International Conference on Mobile, Ubiquitous, and Intelligent Computing (MUSIC). IEEE; 2012, pp. 96-100

[41] Wang Y, Lin W, Zhang T, Ma Y. Research on application and security protection of Internet of things in smart grid; 2012. pp. 1-5

[42] Kiran M, Rajalakshmi P, Bharadwaj K, Acharyya A. Adaptive rule engine based IoT enabled remote healthcare data acquisition and smart transmission system. In: IEEE World Forum on Internet of Things (WF-IoT'14); March 2014. pp. 253-258

[43] Rahmani AM, Thanigaivelan N, Gia TN, Granados J, Negash B, Liljeberg P, et al. Smart e-health gateway: Bringing intelligence to internet-of-things based ubiquitous healthcare systems. In: Consumer Communications and Networking Conference (CCNC), 2015 12th Annual IEEE; Jan 2015. pp. 826-834

[44] EuroTech. Smart Mobility with IoT/M2M Solutions. [Online]. Available from: https://www.eurotech.com/en/ [Accessed: 28 September, 2015]

[45] Kapsch. Driving the future. Powered by kapsch. [Online]. Available from: https://www.kapsch.net/ [Accessed: 28 September, 2015]

[46] Shrouf F, Ordieres J, Miragliotta G. Smart factories in industry 4.0: A review of the concept and of energy management approached in production based on the Internet of things paradigm. In: IEEE International Conference on Industrial Engineering and Engineering Management (IEEM). IEEE; 2014. pp. 697-701

[47] Zhu C, Leung VC, Shu L, Ngai EC-H. Green Internet of things for the smart world. IEEE Access. 2015;**3**:2151-2162

[48] Sala S. Information and communication technologies for climate change adaptation, with a focus on the agricultural sector. In: Thinkpiece for CGIAR Science Forum Workshop

on ICTs Transforming Agricultural Science, Research, And Technology Generation, Wageningen, Netherlands; 2009. pp. 16-17

[49] Eakin H, Wightman PM, Hsu D, Gil Ramón VR, Fuentes-Contreras E, Cox MP, et al. Information and communication technologies and climate change adaptation in Latin America and the Caribbean: A framework for action. Climate and Development. 2015; **7**:208-222

[50] Upadhyay AP, Bijalwan A. Climate change adaptation: Services and role of information communication technology (ICT) in India. American Journal of Environmental Protection. 2015;**4**:70-74

[51] Zanamwe N, Okunoye A. Role of information and communication technologies (ICTs) in mitigating, adapting to and monitoring climate change in developing countries. In: International conference on ICT for Africa; 2013

[52] Mickoleit A. Greener and Smarter: ICTs, the Environment and Climate Change. OECD Publishing; 2010

[53] Di Salvo AL, Agostinho F, Almeida CM, Giannetti BF. Can cloud computing be labeled as "green"? Insights under an environmental accounting perspective. Renewable and Sustainable Energy Reviews. 2017;**69**:514-526

[54] Murugesan S, Harnessing green IT: Principles and practices, IT professional;10; 2008

[55] Rani S, Talwar R, Malhotra J, Ahmed SH, Sarkar M, Song H. A novel scheme for an energy efficient Internet of things based on wireless sensor networks. Sensors. 2015; **15**:28603-28626

[56] Huang J, Meng Y, Gong X, Liu Y, Duan Q. A novel deployment scheme for green Internet of things. IEEE Internet of Things Journal. 2014;**1**:196-205

[57] Gapchup A, Wani A, Wadghule A, Jadhav S. Emerging trends of green IoT for smart world. International Journal of Innovative Research in Computer and Communication Engineering. 2017;**5**:2139-2148

[58] Lü Y-L, Geng J, He G-Z. Industrial transformation and green production to reduce environmental emissions: Taking cement industry as a case. Advances in Climate Change Research. 2015;**6**:202-209

[59] Arshad R, Zahoor S, Shah MA, Wahid A, Yu H. Green IoT: An investigation on energy saving practices for 2020 and beyond. IEEE Access. 2017;**5**:15667-15681

[60] Uddin M, Rahman AA. Energy efficiency and low carbon enabler green IT framework for data centers considering green metrics. Renewable and Sustainable Energy Reviews. 2012;**16**:4078-4094

[61] Xiaojun C, Xianpeng L, Peng X. IOT-based air pollution monitoring and forecasting system. In: 2015 International Conference on Computer and Computational Sciences (ICCCS), IEEE; 2015. pp. 257-260

[62] Manna S, Bhunia SS, Mukherjee N. Vehicular Pollution Monitoring using IoT, Recent Advances and Innovations in Engineering (ICRAIE). IEEE; 2014. pp. 1-5

[63] Zupancic T, Westmacott C, Bulthuis M. The impact of green space on heat and air pollution in urban communities: A meta-narrative systematic review. Vancouver, BC, Canada: David Suzuki Foundation; 2015

[64] Bandyopadhyay D, Sen J. Internet of things: Applications and challenges in technology and standardization. Wireless Personal Communications. 2011;**58**:49-69

[65] Shaikh FK, Zeadally S, Exposito E. Enabling technologies for green Internet of things. IEEE Systems Journal. 2015;**11**:983-994

[66] Murugesan S, Gangadharan G. Harnessing Green IT: Principles and Practices. Chichester, West Sussex, United Kingdom: John Wiley & Sons Ltd; 2012

[67] Nandyala CS, Kim H-K. Green IoT agriculture and healthcare application (GAHA). International Journal of Smart Home. 2016;**10**:289-300